In Flanders Fields

In Flanders Fields

Poetry of the First World War

EDITED BY GEORGE WALTER

8. XII. 05

To John,

With sincere thanks —
for everything!

George

ALLEN LANE
an imprint of
PENGUIN BOOKS

In Memory of Private William Job Packer,
The Royal West Kent Regiment, 1889–1916

ALLEN LANE

Published by the Penguin Group

Penguin Books Ltd, 80 Strand, London WC2R 0RL, England
Penguin Group (USA) Inc., 375 Hudson Street, New York, New York 10014, USA
Penguin Books Australia Ltd, 250 Camberwell Road, Camberwell, Victoria 3124, Australia
Penguin Books Canada Ltd, 10 Alcorn Avenue, Toronto, Ontario, Canada M4V 3B2
Penguin Books India (P) Ltd, 11 Community Centre, Panchsheel Park, New Delhi – 110 017, India
Penguin Books (NZ) Ltd, cnr Airborne and Rosedale Roads, Albany, Auckland 1310, New Zealand
Penguin Books (South Africa) (Pty) Ltd, 24 Sturdee Avenue, Rosebank 2196, South Africa

Penguin Books Ltd, Registered Offices: 80 Strand, London WC2R 0RL, England

www.penguin.com

This collection first published 2004

1

Selection and editorial matter copyright © George Walter, 2004

Pages 366–8 constitute an extension of this copyright page.

The moral right of the editor has been asserted

Set in 9.5/12.5pt Linotype Sabon by Palimpsest Book Production Limited,
Polmont, Stirlingshire
Printed in England by Clays Ltd, St Ives plc

ISBN 0–713–99723–0

Contents

Introduction

'No other class of poetry vanishes so rapidly, has so little chosen from it for posterity.'[1] It seems ironic that this gloomy verdict on the longevity of war poetry should have come from someone who, in time, would come to be regarded as a key contributor to that very genre. But Edward Thomas was writing only months after the outbreak of the First World War, and so can be forgiven for failing to realize that this new war would be unlike all previous wars, not merely in terms of its political, social and cultural impact, but also in terms of the amount of lasting poetry which it would produce. Nor could he have predicted just how popular and widely read this poetry would eventually become. Ninety years later, it's available in some two dozen anthologies, it's studied in schools and in higher education wherever English is taught as a discipline, and it's inspired numerous critical studies, biographies and dramatic and fictional works, and even a series of guidebooks for travellers wishing to re-create the war poets' experiences on the Western Front.[2] Far from vanishing, the poetry of the First World War now has the status of 'a sacred national text'.[3]

Yet, in another sense, Thomas was right. Of the tens of thousands of poems which found their way into print during the war, only a fraction are still being reprinted, and fewer still are read today. It's tempting to argue that this situation is entirely natural, that only the 'best' war poetry has survived the passing of time, but this argument doesn't take into account the crucial role played by anthologists in creating and popularizing what has come to be seen as the canon of First World War poetry. Over the past ninety years there has been a steady stream of collections of war poetry, all of which have sought to introduce readers to the poetic legacy of the war that was meant to end war.[4] Since the 1960s, however, the definition of that legacy and how it should be presented has become somewhat formulaic. Put simply, this has meant that only certain kinds of war poems have been reprinted – the kinds that can be easily arranged in a simplistic narrative expressing 'first of all a naïve enthusiasm for war and then, after the shock of battle experience, an overwhelming sense of disillusion, anger and pity, culminating in pacifism and protest'.[5] There's no doubt that this is a powerful narrative, but it only really reflects the experiences of a handful of those who wrote during the war, and it has created a highly distorted image of what the poetry of the First World War was really like.

This anthology is different. Edmund Blunden evoked the shape-changing god Proteus when struggling to describe the complexity of his wartime experiences,[6] and *In Flanders Fields* reflects this idea in that it offers a much wider range of poems than is usually found in modern selections of war poetry. More importantly, it presents them not in the usual narrative, but rather as a series of thematic groupings. As such, it's probably closer to wartime anthologies such as E. B. Osborn's *The Muse in Arms*[7] than to more recent collections, in that it tries to illustrate the sheer diversity of First World War poetry without arranging that poetry so that it tells a particular story. Instead, I've tried to organize the contents of this book so that the reader is offered a variety of different perspectives on the same common wartime experiences, not merely though the mingling of different voices in each section, but also through the juxtaposition of different sections.

I've tried to be more protean than most recent editors of war poetry, but aesthetic and practical considerations have meant that some kinds of poems have had to be omitted. To give the selection some coherence, I've only drawn upon those poems by combatants which deal with the realities of trench warfare in northern France and Flanders; although other theatres of war such as the Eastern Front and the Dardanelles also had their fair share of poets, it's the Western Front which was and still remains the primary imaginative focus of the First World War. Similarly, I've also chosen not to include any extracts from two of the most sustained poetic responses to the war, T. S. Eliot's *The Waste Land* and David Jones's *In Parenthesis*;[8] given their scale, these two poems really need to be read whole in order to be properly appreciated. In the case of some long sequences of individual poems, however, I've taken the liberty of selecting parts of them on the grounds that these extracts stand alone as complete poems in their own right.

The main part of the anthology is divided into five major sections, each exploring a particular area of wartime experience. The first, *Your Country Needs You*, takes its title from the caption to the famous wartime recruiting poster and brings together the poetic response to the outbreak of the war and the experiences of those ordinary men who 'answered the call' and quickly found themselves in khaki. Within this section, 'Let the foul Scene proceed' presents a selection of reactions to England's declaration of war on Germany in August 1914 and is followed by 'Who's for the khaki suit', which examines the drive for recruitment and the pressures placed on ordinary men to enlist. Finally, 'In Training' deals with the basic training undergone by these men as they prepared for active service: the fatigues, the route marches, the process of embarkation, and then the journey to the war zone.

The second section, *Somewhere in France*, takes its title from a phrase commonly used in soldiers' letters and explores some key aspects of everyday life on the Western Front. 'In Trenches' deals with the experience of being in the front line, and has been loosely arranged to create a picture of a typical day in the trenches. 'Behind the Lines' examines those times when soldiers were in reserve or on rest, and thus had the luxury of observing the delights or otherwise of military life in wartime France. The final subsection, 'Comrades of War', explores one of the central experiences of the Great War for most men: the bonds of friendship and love that were formed between serving men of all ranks. Familiar as this concept may be from the work of officer poets, I've here tried to show that such powerful ties permeated all ranks and were, for many, the most significant of their lives.

Action examines the harsh realities of armed conflict.

'Rendezvous with Death' is a selection of poems giving an insight into what went through the minds of soldiers faced with the possibility of their own impending deaths. As the title suggests, 'Battle' deals with the experience of active warfare; it's arranged so as to give an overview of what happened in any given action, from the laying down of bombardments through the actual fighting itself to its immediate cessation. 'Aftermath' explores the repercussions of any given battle: the sense of relief felt by many at having survived, the experience of the wounded and shell-shocked, and, of course, the presence of the newly dead. This theme is approached not merely through the writing of those who fought, but also through the poetry of those back home in Britain who could only sit and wait for news of their loved ones.

The introduction of the civilian experience of the war in this section forms a bridge with the next, *Blighty*, which looks at serving soldiers' bonds with home and the experience of returning to Britain after active service. 'Going Back' focuses on the conflicts of emotions felt by soldiers returning from the front, whether on leave or because of wounding, while the sense of alienation that some felt is developed in the next section, 'The Other War'. Much of this section explores the sensation that many serving soldiers had of being a race apart when in Blighty, but also emphasizes the point that the war at home was traumatic and difficult for those left behind too. 'Lucky Blighters' is used ironically as the title for the final subsection, of course: while getting 'a Blighty one' was something that many soldiers craved, the poems here show just what the reality was for those so seriously wounded that they could not return to France.

The last major section, *Peace*, examines the end of the war and its aftermath, both short-term and long-term. 'Everyone Sang' explores the personal and political implications of the Armistice, two themes which are developed further in the next section, 'The Dead and the Living'. Here, both public and private commemorations of 'the Million Dead' are juxtaposed with the experience and emotions of those who survived – the widows, the grieving parents, and the demobilized. 'Have you forgotten yet?' explores the long-term impact of the war on its survivors, showing the variety of ways in which the war continued to permeate the work of these veterans throughout the 1920s and 1930s.

The anthology as a whole is framed by two single poems. A. E. Housman's 'On the idle hill of summer' serves as a kind of prelude, introducing not only the major themes of the collection, but also the rhetoric and stylistic patterning present in so much First World War poetry; Housman's *A Shropshire Lad*[9] was a wartime best-seller, and its influence, in terms of both form and content, can be found everywhere in the poetry of the period. As a coda I've included Edmund Blunden's 'Ancre Sunshine'; written in 1966, this appears to be the last poem that Blunden wrote, and also the last war poem to be published by any survivor of the war. As such, it seems to me to be a highly fitting way to end this selection.

The last word should perhaps be left to Charles Carrington. A survivor of both the Somme and

Passchendaele offensives, he lived to see the protean war he had fought in become distorted almost out of all recognition:

Just smile and make an old soldier's wry joke when you see yourself on the television screen, agonized and woebegone, trudging from disaster to disaster, knee-deep in moral as well as physical mud, hesitant about your purpose, submissive to a harsh, irrelevant discipline, mistrustful of your commanders. Is it any use to assert that I was not like that, and my dead friends were not like that, and the old cronies I meet at reunions are not like that?[10]

I hope it's not too presumptive of me to hope that he would have found the war depicted in this selection of poems a lot more recognizable.

Notes

1. Edward Thomas, 'War Poetry', *Poetry and Drama*, 2, 8 (December 1914), p. 341.
2. The most recent volume in this series is Helen McPhail and Philip Guest's *Sassoon and Graves: On the Trail of the Poets of the Great War* (London: Leo Cooper, 2001).
3. Andrew Motion, 'Introduction', *First World War Poems* (London: Faber & Faber, 2003), p. xi.
4. This well-known formula is derived from H. G. Wells's *The War That Will End War* (London: F. & C. Palmer, 1914).
5. Andrew Rutherford, *The Literature of War: Five Studies in Heroic Virtue* (London: Macmillan, 1978), p. 65.

6. See his letter of 31 March 1918 in Barry Webb's *Edmund Blunden: A Biography* (New Haven and London: Yale University Press, 1990), p. 46. He used the same image over a decade later in his introduction to Frederic Brereton's *An Anthology of War Poems* (London: Collins, 1930), where he wrote, 'The face of war is one of protean changes. In order to catch those countenances, a man has to be acute in a rare degree' (p. 20).

7. E. B. Osborn, ed., *The Muse in Arms: A Collection of War Poems, for the Most Part Written in the Field of Action, by Seamen, Soldiers and Flying Men Who Are Serving, or Have Served in the Great War* (London: John Murray, 1917).

8. T. S. Eliot, *The Waste Land* (New York: Boni & Liveright, 1922); David Jones, *In Parenthesis* (London: Faber & Faber, 1937).

9. A. E. Housman, *A Shropshire Lad* (London: Kegan Paul & Co., 1896).

10. Quoted in Martin Stephen's *The Price of Pity: Poetry, History and Myth in the Great War* (London: Leo Cooper, 1996), p. 78.

Acknowledgements

I wish to thank the staff of the British Library, the Bodleian Library in Oxford, Birmingham Central Library and the University of Sussex Library for their help during the early stages of this edition. I am also very grateful to the English Department at the University of Sussex for providing me with two very able and enthusiastic research assistants: Catherine Ezzo, whose help with the preparation of the texts was invaluable, and Esther MacCallum-Stewart, whose contribution during the final stages of this book went well beyond that of a research assistant; indeed, her knowledge of the subject and enthusiasm for the project meant that, at times, working with her felt more like a collaboration – and a very enjoyable one at that.

I am grateful to friends and colleagues at the universities of Birmingham and Sussex for their willingness to share their ideas and to allow me to test my own: R. K. R. Thornton, Steve Ellis, Tony Inglis, Norman Vance, Philippa Lyon, and particularly John Jacobs and Rodney Hillman. John and Rodney's comments on an early draft of the anthology were invaluable, and their support and encouragement throughout the project are much appreciated. Thanks are also due to Essaka Joshua and Fuyubi Nakamura for their willingness to source and retrieve a number of particularly elusive texts. I would also like to acknowledge the very real contribution which my students, both undergraduate and postgraduate, made to the final shape of this book; in particular, I am very grateful to Martyn Oliver, Ben Scott, Helen Tripp and Dendi Wolffsky-Batson for their comments and ideas. My editors at Penguin also deserve a considerable vote of thanks, especially Martin Toseland and Bob Davenport, whose enthusiasm, patience and support during the latter stages of the book was admirable.

My personal thanks go to all those who, in various ways, have ensured the completion of this book: Christine Munday, David and Tracy Buxton, Jon and Hildi Mitchell, Linda MacCallum-Stewart and especially Anne Johnson, without whose help and support I would not have been able to create this anthology. My original intention was to dedicate this to my mother and stepfather, Sandra and Dennis O'Leary, in recognition of the love and support they have given and continue to give me. I hope when they see the dedication they will understand why I have changed it and why, in a sense, my original dedication to them still stands.

A Note on the Text

My copy-text for the poems in *In Flanders Fields* has been, in every case, their first publication in book form, on the grounds that this is most likely to represent the author's intentions at the point at which he or she wished to place their work before the public. All too often these early versions were subsequently revised, but I've preferred the earlier texts, because they reflect the authors' intentions at a specific historical moment – usually during the war or shortly afterwards (and in many cases they are the versions of poems which made a particular poet's reputation).

Of course, some of the poets I've included didn't live to revise their work. In these cases I have again used the first book printing of a poem as my copy-text, even when subsequent posthumous editions have shown these early texts to be flawed; this sometimes results in unfamiliar versions of familiar poems, but it does have the advantage of creating a historically coherent edition and, more importantly, it allows the reader to encounter these poems in the form in which they were first read.

On the whole, the texts have been reproduced as they originally appeared, retaining all the quirks of spelling, punctuation and capitalization which characterize the poetry of this period. However, in line with modern publishing conventions, the indication of section breaks within poems and the style of quotation marks, ellipses

and dashes have been standardized. It was common prac-
tice to append dates and locations to poems during the
war; these can now be found in the Notes.

PRELUDE

'On the idle hill of summer'

On the idle hill of summer,
    Sleepy with the flow of streams,
Far I hear the steady drummer
    Drumming like a noise in dreams.

Far and near and low and louder
    On the roads of earth go by,
Dear to friends and food for powder,
    Soldiers marching, all to die.

East and west on fields forgotten
    Bleach the bones of comrades slain,   10
Lovely lads and dead and rotten;
    None that go return again.

Far the calling bugles hollo,
    High the screaming fife replies,
Gay the files of scarlet follow:
    Woman bore me, I will rise.

A. E. Housman

'Let the foul Scene proceed'

Channel Firing

That night your great guns, unawares,
Shook all our coffins as we lay,
And broke the chancel window-squares,
We thought it was the Judgement-day

And sat upright. While drearisome
Arose the howl of wakened hounds:
The mouse let fall the altar-crumb,
The worms drew back into the mounds,

The glebe-cow drooled. Till God called, 'No;
It's gunnery practice out at sea   10
Just as before you went below;
The world is as it used to be:

'All nations striving strong to make
Red war yet redder. Mad as hatters
They do no more for Christés sake
Than you who are helpless in such matters.

'That this is not the judgement-hour
For some of them's a blessed thing,
For if it were they'd have to scour
Hell's floor for so much threatening . . .   20

'Ha, ha. It will be warmer when
I blow the trumpet (if indeed
I ever do; for you are men,
And rest eternal sorely need).'

So down we lay again. 'I wonder,
Will the world ever saner be,'
Said one, 'than when He sent us under
In our indifferent century!'

And many a skeleton shook his head.
'Instead of preaching forty year,'   30
My neighbour Parson Thirdly said,
'I wish I had stuck to pipes and beer.'

Again the guns disturbed the hour,
Roaring their readiness to avenge,
As far inland as Stourton Tower,
And Camelot, and starlit Stonehenge.

Thomas Hardy

The Eve of War

The night falls over London. City and sky
  Blend slowly. All the crowded plain grows dark.
  The last few loiterers leave the glooming park
To swell that mighty tide which still sweeps by,
Heedless save of its own humanity,
  Down to the Circus, where the staring arc
  Winks through the night, and every face shows stark
And every cheek betrays its painted lie.

But here through bending trees blows a great wind;
  Through torn cloud-gaps the angry stars
    look down.   10
Here have I heard this night the wings of War,
His dark and frowning countenance I saw.
  What dreadful menace hangs above our town?
Let all the great cities pray; for they have sinned.

Geoffrey Faber

On Receiving the First News of the War

Snow is a strange white word;
No ice or frost
Has asked of bud or bird
For Winter's cost.

Yet ice and frost and snow
From earth to sky
This Summer land doth know;
No man knows why.

In all men's hearts it is:
Some spirit old
Hath turned with malign kiss
Our lives to mould.

Red fangs have torn His face,
God's blood is shed:
He mourns from His lone place
His children dead.

O ancient crimson curse!
Corrode, consume;
Give back this universe
Its pristine bloom.

Isaac Rosenberg

The Marionettes

Let the foul Scene proceed:
    There's laughter in the wings;
'Tis sawdust that they bleed,
    But a box Death brings.

How rare a skill is theirs
    These extreme pangs to show,
How real a frenzy wears
    Each feigner of woe!

Gigantic dins uprise!
    Even the gods must feel
A smarting of the eyes
    As these fumes upsweal.

Strange, such a Piece is free,
    While we Spectators sit,
Aghast at its agony,
    Yet absorbed in it!

Dark is the outer air,
    Coldly the night draughts blow,
Mutely we stare, and stare
    At the frenzied Show.

Yet heaven hath its quiet shroud
    Of deep, immutable blue –
We cried 'An end!' We are bowed
    By the dread, ''Tis true!'

While the Shape who hoofs applause
    Behind our deafened ear,
Hoots – angel-wise – 'the Cause!'
    And affrights ev'n fear.

Walter de la Mare

August, 1914

How still this quiet cornfield is to-night!
By an intenser glow the evening falls,
Bringing, not darkness, but a deeper light;
Among the stooks a partridge covey calls.

The windows glitter on the distant hill;
Beyond the hedge the sheep-bells in the fold
Stumble on sudden music and are still;
The forlorn pinewoods droop above the wold.

An endless quiet valley reaches out
Past the blue hills into the evening sky;   10
Over the stubble, cawing, goes a rout
Of rooks from harvest, flagging as they fly.

So beautiful it is, I never saw
So great a beauty on these English fields
Touched by the twilight's coming into awe,
Ripe to the soul and rich with summer's yields.

                              *

These homes, this valley spread below me here,
The rooks, the tilted stacks, the beasts in pen,
Have been the heartfelt things, past-speaking dear
To unknown generations of dead men,   20

Who, century after century, held these farms,
And, looking out to watch the changing sky,

Heard, as we hear, the rumours and alarms
Of war at hand and danger pressing nigh.

And knew, as we know, that the message meant
The breaking-off of ties, the loss of friends,
Death like a miser getting in his rent,
And no new stones laid where the trackway ends.

The harvest not yet won, the empty bin,
The friendly horses taken from the stalls,   30
The fallow on the hill not yet brought in,
The cracks unplastered in the leaking walls.

Yet heard the news, and went discouraged home,
And brooded by the fire with heavy mind,
With such dumb loving of the Berkshire loam
As breaks the dumb hearts of the English kind,

Then sadly rose and left the well-loved Downs,
And so, by ship to sea, and knew no more
The fields of home, the byres, the market towns,
Nor the dear outline of the English shore,   40

But knew the misery of the soaking trench,
The freezing in the rigging, the despair
In the revolting second of the wrench
When the blind soul is flung upon the air,

And died (uncouthly, most) in foreign lands
For some idea but dimly understood
Of an English city never built by hands
Which love of England prompted and made good.

If there be any life beyond the grave,
It must be near the men and things we love,   50
Some power of quick suggestion how to save,
Touching the living soul as from above.

An influence from the Earth from those dead hearts
So passionate once, so deep, so truly kind,
That in the living child the spirit starts,
Feeling companioned still, not left behind.

Surely above these fields a spirit broods
A sense of many watchers muttering near
Of the lone Downland with the forlorn woods
Loved to the death, inestimably dear.   60

A muttering from beyond the veils of Death
From long dead men, to whom this quiet scene
Came among blinding tears with the last breath,
The dying soldier's vision of his queen.

All the unspoken worship of those lives
Spent in forgotten wars at other calls
Glimmers upon these fields where evening drives
Beauty like breath, so gently darkness falls.

Darkness that makes the meadows holier still,
The elm trees sadden in the hedge, a sigh   70
Moves in the beech-clump on the haunted hill,
The rising planets deepen in the sky,

And silence broods like spirit on the brae,
A glimmering moon begins, the moonlight runs
Over the grasses of the ancient way
Rutted this morning by the passing guns.

John Masefield

1914: *Peace*

Now, God be thanked Who has matched us with His
      hour,
  And caught our youth, and wakened us from
      sleeping,
With hand made sure, clear eye, and sharpened power,
  To turn, as swimmers into cleanness leaping,
Glad from a world grown old and cold and weary,
  Leave the sick hearts that honour could not move,
And half-men, and their dirty songs and dreary,
  And all the little emptiness of love!

Oh! we, who have known shame, we have found
      release there,
  Where there's no ill, no grief, but sleep has
      mending,   10
    Naught broken save this body, lost but breath;
Nothing to shake the laughing heart's long peace there
  But only agony, and that has ending;
    And the worst friend and enemy is but Death.

Rupert Brooke

Happy is England Now

There is not anything more wonderful
Than a great people moving towards the deep
Of an unguessed and unfeared future; nor
Is aught so dear of all held dear before
As the new passion stirring in their veins
When the destroying Dragon wakes from sleep.

Happy is England now, as never yet!
And though the sorrows of the slow days fret
Her faithfullest children, grief itself is proud.
Ev'n the warm beauty of this spring and summer   10
That turns to bitterness turns then to gladness
Since for this England the beloved ones died.

Happy is England in the brave that die
For wrongs not hers and wrongs so sternly hers;
Happy in those that give, give, and endure
The pain that never the new years may cure;
Happy in all her dark woods, green fields, towns,
Her hills and rivers and her chafing sea.

What'er was dear before is dearer now.
There's not a bird singing upon his bough   20
But sings the sweeter in our English ears:
There's not a nobleness of heart, hand, brain
But shines the purer; happy is England now
In those that fight, and watch with pride and tears.

John Freeman

'For All We Have and Are'
1914

For all we have and are,
For all our children's fate,
Stand up and take the war,
The Hun is at the gate!
Our world has passed away,
In wantonness o'erthrown.
There is nothing left to-day
But steel and fire and stone!
   Though all we knew depart,
   The old Commandments stand: –   10
   'In courage keep your heart,
   In strength lift up your hand.'

Once more we hear the word
That sickened earth of old: –
'No law except the Sword
Unsheathed and uncontrolled.'
Once more it knits mankind,
Once more the nations go
To meet and break and bind
A crazed and driven foe.   20

Comfort, content, delight,
The ages' slow-bought gain,
They shrivelled in a night.
Only ourselves remain
To face the naked days
In silent fortitude,

Through perils and dismays
Renewed and re-renewed.
    Though all we made depart,
    The old Commandments stand: –   30
    'In patience keep your heart,
    In strength lift up your hand.'

No easy hope or lies
Shall bring us to our goal,
But iron sacrifice
Of body, will, and soul.
There is but one task for all –
One life for each to give.
Who stands if Freedom fall?
Who dies if England live?   40

Rudyard Kipling

This is no case of petty Right or Wrong

This is no case of petty right or wrong
That politicians or philosophers
Can judge. I hate not Germans, nor grow hot
With love of Englishmen, to please newspapers.
Beside my hate for one fat patriot
My hatred of the Kaiser is love true: –
A kind of god he is, banging a gong.
But I have not to choose between the two,
Or between justice and injustice. Dinned
With war and argument I read no more   10
Than in the storm smoking along the wind
Athwart the wood. Two witches' cauldrons roar.
From one the weather shall rise clear and gay;
Out of the other an England beautiful
And like her mother that died yesterday.
Little I know or care if, being dull,
I shall miss something that historians
Can rake out of the ashes when perchance
The phoenix broods serene above their ken.
But with the best and meanest Englishmen   20
I am one in crying, God save England, lest
We lose what never slaves and cattle blessed.
The ages made her that made us from dust:
She is all we know and live by, and we trust
She is good and must endure, loving her so:
And as we love ourselves we hate her foe.

Edward Thomas

To Germany

You are blind like us. Your hurt no man designed,
And no man claimed the conquest of your land.
But gropers both through fields of thought confined
We stumble and we do not understand.
You only saw your future bigly planned,
And we, the tapering paths of our own mind,
And in each other's dearest ways we stand,
And hiss and hate. And the blind fight the blind.

When it is peace, then we may view again
With new-won eyes each other's truer form   10
And wonder. Grown more loving-kind and warm
We'll grasp firm hands and laugh at the old pain,
When it is peace. But until peace, the storm
The darkness and the thunder and the rain.

Charles Hamilton Sorley

The Poets are Waiting

To what God
Shall we chant
Our songs of Battle?

The professional poets
Are measuring their thoughts
For felicitous sonnets;
They try them and fit them
Like honest tailors
Cutting materials
For fashion-plate suits.   10

The unprofessional
Little singers,
Most intellectual,
Merry with gossip,
Heavy with cunning,
Whose tedious brains are draped
In sultry palls of hair,
Reclining as usual
On armchairs and sofas,
Are grinning and gossiping,   20
Cake at their elbows –
They will not write us verses for the time;
Their storms are brewed in teacups and their wars
Are fought in sneers or little blots of ink.

To what God
Shall we chant
Our songs of Battle?

Hefty barbarians,
Roaring for war,
Are breaking upon us;   30
Clouds of their cavalry,
Waves of their infantry,
Mountains of guns.
Winged they are coming,
Plated and mailed,
Snorting their jargon.
Oh to whom shall a song of battle be chanted?

Not to our lord of the hosts on his ancient throne,
Drowsing the ages out in Heaven
The celestial choirs are mute, the angels have fled: 40
Word is gone forth abroad that our lord is dead.

To what God shall we chant
Our songs
Of battle?

Harold Monro

The Dilemma

God heard the embattled nations sing and shout
'Gott strafe England!' and 'God save the King!'
God this, God that, and God the other thing –
'Good God!' said God 'I've got my work cut out.'

J. C. Squire

'Who's for the khaki suit'

The Trumpet

Rise up, rise up,
And, as the trumpet blowing
Chases the dreams of men,
As the dawn glowing
The stars that left unlit
The land and water,
Rise up and scatter
The dew that covers
The print of last night's lovers –
Scatter it, scatter it!   10

While you are listening
To the clear horn,
Forget, men, everything
On this earth newborn,
Except that it is lovelier
Than any mysteries.
Open your eyes to the air
That has washed the eyes of the stars
Through all the dewy night:
Up with the light,   20
To the old wars;
Arise, arise!

Edward Thomas

The Call

Who's for the trench –
    Are you, my laddie?
Who'll follow French –
    Will you, my laddie?
Who's fretting to begin,
Who's going out to win?
And who wants to save his skin –
    Do you, my laddie?

Who's for the khaki suit –
    Are you, my laddie?
Who longs to charge and shoot –
    Do you, my laddie?
Who's keen on getting fit,
Who means to show his grit,
And who'd rather wait a bit –
    Would you, my laddie?

Who'll earn the Empire's thanks –
    Will you, my laddie?
Who'll swell the victor's ranks –
    Will you, my laddie?
When that procession comes,
Banners and rolling drums –
Who'll stand and bite his thumbs –
    Will you, my laddie?

Jessie Pope

Recruiting

'Lads, you're wanted, go and help,'
On the railway carriage wall
Stuck the poster, and I thought
Of the hands that penned the call.

Fat civilians wishing they
'Could go out and fight the Hun.'
Can't you see them thanking God
That they're over forty-one?

Girls with feathers, vulgar songs –
Washy verse on England's need –   10
God – and don't we damned well know
How the message ought to read.

'Lads, you're wanted! over there,'
Shiver in the morning dew,
More poor devils like yourselves
Waiting to be killed by you.

Go and help to swell the names
In the casualty lists.
Help to make a column's stuff
For the blasted journalists.   20

Help to keep them nice and safe
From the wicked German foe.
Don't let him come over here!
'Lads, you're wanted – out you go.'

There's a better word than that,
Lads, and can't you hear it come
From a million men that call
You to share their martyrdom.

Leave the harlots still to sing
Comic songs about the Hun,   30
Leave the fat old men to say
Now *we've* got them on the run.

Better twenty honest years
Than their dull three score and ten.
Lads, you're wanted. Come and learn
To live and die with honest men.

You shall learn what men can do
If you will but pay the price,
Learn the gaiety and strength
In the gallant sacrifice.   40

Take your risk of life and death
Underneath the open sky.
Live clean or go out quick –
Lads, you're wanted. Come and die.

E. A. Mackintosh

Soldier: Twentieth Century

I love you, great new Titan!
Am I not you?
Napoleon and Caesar
Out of you grew.

Out of unthinkable torture,
Eyes kissed by death,
Won back to the world again,
Lost and won in a breath,

Cruel men are made immortal,
Out of your pain born.   10
They have stolen the sun's power
With their feet on your shoulders worn.

Let them shrink from your girth,
That has outgrown the pallid days,
When you slept like Circe's swine,
Or a word in the brain's ways.

Isaac Rosenberg

Youth in Arms I

Happy boy, happy boy,
David the immortal-willed,
Youth a thousand thousand times
Slain, but not once killed,
Swaggering again to-day
In the old contemptuous way;

Leaning backward from your thigh
Up against the tinselled bar –
Dust and ashes! is it you?
Laughing, boasting, there you are!   10
First we hardly recognised you
In your modern avatar.

Soldier, rifle, brown khaki –
Is your blood as happy so?
Where's your sling, or painted shield,
Helmet, pike, or bow?
Well, you're going to the wars –
That is all you need to know.

Greybeards plotted. They were sad.
Death was in their wrinkled eyes.   20
At their tables, with their maps
Plans and calculations, wise
They all seemed; for well they knew
How ungrudgingly Youth dies.

At their green official baize
They debated all the night
Plans for your adventurous days,
Which you followed with delight,
Youth in all your wanderings,
David of a thousand slings.   30

Harold Monro

'I don't want to be a soldier'

I don't want to be a soldier,
I don't want to go to war.
I'd rather stay at home,
Around the streets to roam,
And live on the earnings of a well-paid whore.
I don't want a bayonet up my arsehole,
I don't want my bollocks shot away.
I'd rather stay in England,
In merry, merry England,
And fuck my bleeding life away.   10

Soldiers' song

The Conscript

Indifferent, flippant, earnest, but all bored,
The doctors sit in the glare of electric light
Watching the endless stream of naked white
Bodies of men for whom their hasty award
Means life or death, maybe, or the living death
Of mangled limbs, blind eyes, or a darkened brain;
And the chairman, as his monocle falls again,
Pronounces each doom with easy indifferent breath.

Then suddenly I shudder as I see
A young man stand before them wearily,   10
Cadaverous as one already dead;
But still they stare, untroubled, as he stands
With arms outstretched and drooping thorn-crowned
    head,
The nail-marks glowing in his feet and hands.

Wilfrid Gibson

Rondeau of a Conscientious Objector

The hours have tumbled their leaden, monotonous
   sands
And piled them up in a dull grey heap in the West.
I carry my patience sullenly through the waste lands;
To-morrow will pour them all back, the dull hours I
   detest.

I force my cart through the sodden filth that is pressed
Into ooze, and the sombre dirt spouts up at my hands
As I make my way in twilight now to rest.
The hours have tumbled their leaden, monotonous
   sands.

A twisted thorn-tree still in the evening stands
Defending the memory of leaves and the happy round
   nest.   10
But mud has flooded the homes of these weary lands
And piled them up in a dull grey heap in the West.

All day has the clank of iron on iron distressed
The nerve-bare place. Now a little silence expands
And a gasp of relief. But the soul is still compressed:
I carry my patience sullenly through the waste lands.

The hours have ceased to fall, and a star commands
Shadows to cover our stricken manhood, and blest
Sleep to make forget: but he understands:
To-morrow will pour them all back, the dull hours I
    detest.   20

D. H. Lawrence

1914: Safety

Dear! of all happy in the hour, most blest
    He who has found our hid security,
Assured in the dark tides of the world that rest,
    And heard our word, 'Who is so safe as we?'
We have found safety with all things undying,
    The winds, and morning, tears of men and mirth,
The deep night, and birds singing, and clouds flying,
    And sleep, and freedom, and the autumnal earth.
We have built a house that is not for Time's throwing.
    We have gained a peace unshaken by pain
        for ever.   10
War knows no power. Safe shall be my going,
    Secretly armed against all death's endeavour;
Safe though all safety's lost; safe where men fall;
And if these poor limbs die, safest of all.

Rupert Brooke

'Now that you too must shortly go the way'

Now that you too must shortly go the way
Which in these bloodshot years uncounted men
Have gone in vanishing armies day by day,
And in their numbers will not come again:
I must not strain the moments of our meeting
Striving each look, each accent, not to miss,
Or question of our parting and our greeting,
Is this the last of all? is this – or this?

Last sight of all it may be with these eyes,
Last touch, last hearing, since eyes, hands, and ears,   10
Even serving love, are our mortalities,
And cling to what they own in mortal fears: –
But oh, let end what will, I hold you fast
By immortal love, which has no first or last.

Eleanor Farjeon

In Training

The Kiss

To these I turn, in these I trust;
Brother Lead and Sister Steel.
To his blind power I make appeal;
I guard her beauty clean from rust.

He spins and burns and loves the air,
And splits a skull to win my praise;
But up the nobly marching days
She glitters naked, cold and fair.

Sweet Sister, grant your soldier this;
That in good fury he may feel   10
The body where he sets his heel
Quail from your downward darting kiss.

Siegfried Sassoon

Arms and the Boy

Let the boy try along this bayonet-blade
How cold steel is, and keen with hunger of blood;
Blue with all malice, like a madman's flash;
And thinly drawn with famishing for flesh.

Lend him to stroke these blind, blunt bullet-heads
Which long to muzzle in the hearts of lads.
Or give him cartridges of fine zinc teeth,
Sharp with the sharpness of grief and death.

For his teeth seem for laughing round an apple.
There lurk no claws behind his fingers supple;   10
And God will grow no talons at his heels,
Nor antlers through the thickness of his curls.

Wilfred Owen

'All the hills and vales along'

All the hills and vales along
Earth is bursting into song,
And the singers are the chaps
Who are going to die perhaps.
    O sing, marching men,
    Till the valleys ring again.
    Give your gladness to earth's keeping,
    So be glad, when you are sleeping.

Cast away regret and rue,
Think what you are marching to.   10
Little live, great pass.
Jesus Christ and Barabbas
Were found the same day.
This died, that went his way.
    So sing with joyful breath,
    For why, you are going to death.
    Teeming earth will surely store
    All the gladness that you pour.

Earth that never doubts nor fears,
Earth that knows of death, not tears,   20
Earth that bore with joyful ease
Hemlock for Socrates,
Earth that blossomed and was glad
'Neath the cross that Christ had,
Shall rejoice and blossom too
When the bullet reaches you.
    Wherefore, men marching

On the road to death, sing!
Pour gladness on earth's head,
So be merry, so be dead.   30

From the hills and valleys earth
Shouts back the sound of mirth,
Tramp of feet and lilt of song
Ringing all the road along.
All the music of their going,
Ringing swinging glad song-throwing,
Earth will echo still, when foot
Lies numb and voice mute.
    On, marching men, on
    To the gates of death with song.   40
    Sow your gladness for earth's reaping,
    So you may be glad, though sleeping.
    Strew your gladness on earth's bed,
    So be merry, so be dead.

Charles Hamilton Sorley

'We are Fred Karno's army'

We are Fred Karno's army, we are the ragtime infantry.
We cannot fight, we cannot shoot, what bleeding use
    are we?
And when we get to Berlin we'll hear the Kaiser say,
'Hoch! Hoch! Mein Gott, what a bloody rotten lot are
    the ragtime infantry.'

Soldiers' song

Song of the Dark Ages

We digged our trenches on the down
   Beside old barrows, and the wet
White chalk we shovelled from below;
It lay like drifts of thawing snow
   On parados and parapet:

Until a pick neither struck flint
   Nor split the yielding chalky soil,
But only calcined human bone:
Poor relic of that Age of Stone
   Whose ossuary was our spoil.   10

Home we marched singing in the rain,
   And all the while, beneath our song,
I mused how many springs should wane
And still our trenches scar the plain:
   The monument of an old wrong.

But then, I thought, the fair green sod
   Will wholly cover that white stain,
And soften, as it clothes the face
Of those old barrows, every trace
   Of violence to the patient plain.   20

And careless people, passing by
   Will speak of both in casual tone:
Saying: 'You see the toil they made:
The age of iron, pick and spade,
   Here jostles with the Age of Stone.'

Yet either from that happier race
    Will merit but a passing glance;
And they will leave us both alone:
Poor savages who wrought in stone –
    Poor savages who fought in France.   30

Francis Brett Young

Sonnets 1917: Servitude

If it were not for England, who would bear
This heavy servitude one moment more?
To keep a brothel, sweep and wash the floor
Of filthiest hovels were noble to compare
With this brass-cleaning life. Now here, now there
Harried in foolishness, scanned curiously o'er
By fools made brazen by conceit, and store
Of antique witticisms thin and bare.

Only the love of comrades sweetens all,
Whose laughing spirit will not be outdone.   10
As night-watching men wait for the sun
To hearten them, so wait I on such boys
As neither brass nor Hell-fire may appal,
Nor guns, nor sergeant-major's bluster and noise.

Ivor Gurney

In Barracks

The barrack-square, washed clean with rain,
Shines wet and wintry-grey and cold.
Young Fusiliers, strong-legged and bold,
March and wheel and march again.
The sun looks over the barrack gate,
Warm and white with glaring shine,
To watch the soldiers of the Line
That life has hired to fight with fate.

Fall out: the long parades are done.
Up comes the dark; down goes the sun.   10
The square is walled with windowed light.
Sleep well, you lusty Fusiliers;
Shut your brave eyes on sense and sight,
And banish from your dreamless ears
The bugle's dying notes that say,
'Another night; another day.'

Siegfried Sassoon

The Last Post

The bugler sent a call of high romance –
'Lights out! Lights out!' to the deserted square.
On the thin brazen notes he threw a prayer,
'God, if it's *this* for me next time in France . . .
O spare the phantom bugle as I lie
Dead in the gas and smoke and roar of guns,
Dead in a row with the other broken ones
Lying so stiff and still under the sky,
Jolly young Fusiliers too good to die.'

Robert Graves

In Training

The wind is cold and heavy
   And storms are in the sky:
Our path across the heather
   Goes higher and more high.

To right, the town we came from,
   To left, blue hills and sea:
The wind is growing colder
   And shivering are we.

We drag with stiffening fingers
   Our rifles up the hill.   10
The path is steep and tangled
   But leads to Flanders still.

Edward Shanks

Youth in Arms II: Soldier

Are you going? To-night we must hear all your
    laughter;
We shall need to remember it in the quiet days after.
Lift your rough hands, grained like unpolished oak.
Drink, call, lean forward, tell us some happy joke.
Let us know every whim of your brain and innocent
    soul.
Your speech is let loose; your great loafing words roll
Like hill-waters. But every syllable said
Brings you nearer the time you'll be found lying dead
In a ditch, or rolled stiff on the stones of a plain.
(Thought! Thought go back into your kennel again: 10
Hound, back!) Drink your glass, happy soldier, to-night.
Death is quick; you will laugh as you march to the
    fight.
We are wrong. Dreaming ever, we falter and pause:
You go forward unharmed without Why or Because.
Spring does not question. The war is like rain;
You will fall in the field like a flower without pain;
And who shall have noticed one sweet flower that dies?
The rain comes; the leaves open, and other flowers rise.

Harold Monro

'Men Who March Away'
(Song of the Soldiers)

What of the faith and fire within us
      Men who march away
      Ere the barn-cocks say
      Night is growing gray,
To hazards whence no tears can win us;
What of the faith and fire within us
      Men who march away!

Is it a purblind prank, O think you,
      Friend with the musing eye
      Who watch us stepping by   10
      With doubt and dolorous sigh?
Can much pondering so hoodwink you?
Is it a purblind prank, O think you,
      Friend with the musing eye?

Nay. We see well what we are doing,
      Though some may not see –
      Dalliers as they be –
      England's need are we;
Her distress would leave us rueing:
Nay. We well see what we are doing,   20
      Though some may not see!

In our heart of hearts believing
      Victory crowns the just,
      And that braggarts must
      Surely bite the dust,
Press we to the field ungrieving,
In our heart of hearts believing
      Victory crowns the just.

Hence the faith and fire within us
      Men who march away   30
      Ere the barn-cocks say
      Night is growing gray,
To hazards whence no tears can win us;
Hence the faith and fire within us
      Men who march away.

Thomas Hardy

Marching Men

Under the level winter sky
I saw a thousand Christs go by.
They sang an idle song and free
As they went up to calvary.

Careless of eye and coarse of lip,
They marched in holiest fellowship.
That heaven might heal the world, they gave
Their earth-born dreams to deck the grave.

With souls unpurged and steadfast breath
They supped the sacrament of death.   10
And for each one, far off, apart,
Seven swords have rent a woman's heart.

Marjorie Pickthall

The Send-off

Down the close, darkening lanes they sang their way
To the siding-shed,
And lined the train with faces grimly gay.

Their breasts were stuck all white with wreath and
  spray
As men's are, dead.

Dull porters watched them, and a casual tramp
Stood staring hard,
Sorry to miss them from the upland camp.
Then, unmoved, signals nodded, and a lamp
Winked to the guard.   10

So secretly, like wrongs hushed-up, they went.
They were not ours:
We never heard to which front these were sent.

Nor there if they yet mock what women meant
Who gave them flowers.

Shall they return to beatings of great bells
In wild trainloads?
A few, a few, too few for drums and yells,
May creep back, silent, to still village wells
Up half-known roads.   20

Wilfred Owen

Fragment

I strayed about the deck, an hour, to-night
Under a cloudy moonless sky; and peeped
In at the windows, watched my friends at table,
Or playing cards, or standing in the doorway,
Or coming out into the darkness. Still
No one could see me.

                    I would have thought of them
– Heedless, within a week of battle – in pity,
Pride in their strength and in the weight and firmness
And link'd beauty of bodies, and pity that
This gay machine of splendour'ld soon be broken,   10
Thought little of, pashed, scattered . . .

                    Only, always,
I could but see them – against the lamplight – pass
Like coloured shadows, thinner than filmy glass,
Slight bubbles, fainter than the wave's faint light,
That broke to phosphorus out in the night,
Perishing things and strange ghosts – soon to die
To other ghosts – this one, or that, or I.

Rupert Brooke

45

2 SOMEWHERE IN FRANCE

In Trenches

First Time In

After the dread tales and red yarns of the Line
Anything might have come to us; but the divine
Afterglow brought us up to a Welsh colony
Hiding in sandbag ditches, whispering consolatory
Soft foreign things. Then we were taken in
To low huts candle-lit, shaded close by slitten
Oilsheets, and there the boys gave us kind
    welcome,
So that we looked out as from the edge of home.
Sang us Welsh things, and changed all former
    notions
To human hopeful things. And the next
    day's guns   10
Nor any line-pangs ever quite could blot out
That strangely beautiful entry to war's rout;
Candles they gave us, precious and shared over-
    rations –
Ulysses found little more in his wanderings without
    doubt.

'David of the White Rock', the 'Slumber Song' so
  soft, and that
Beautiful tune to which roguish words by Welsh pit
  boys
Are sung – but never more beautiful than here under
  the guns' noise.

Ivor Gurney

Break of Day in the Trenches

The darkness crumbles away –
It is the same old druid Time as ever.
Only a live thing leaps my hand –
A queer sardonic rat –
As I pull the parapet's poppy
To stick behind my ear.
Droll rat, they would shoot you if they knew
Your cosmopolitan sympathies
(And God knows what antipathies).
Now you have touched this English hand   10
You will do the same to a German –
Soon, no doubt, if it be your pleasure
To cross the sleeping green between.
It seems you inwardly grin as you pass
Strong eyes, fine limbs, haughty athletes
Less chanced than you for life,
Bonds to the whims of murder,
Sprawled in the bowels of the earth,
The torn fields of France.
What do you see in our eyes   20
At the shrieking iron and flame
Hurled through still heavens?
What quaver – what heart aghast?
Poppies whose roots are in man's veins
Drop, and are ever dropping;
But mine in my ear is safe,
Just a little white with the dust.

Isaac Rosenberg

'Bombed last night'

Bombed last night, and bombed the night before.
Going to get bombed tonight if we never get bombed
   any more.
When we're bombed, we're scared as we can be.
Can't stop the bombing from old Higher Germany.

They're warning us, they're warning us.
One shell hole for just the four of us.
Thank your lucky stars there are no more of us.
So one of us can fill it all alone.

Gassed last night, and gassed the night before.
Going to get gassed tonight if we never get gassed
   any more.   10
When we're gassed, we're sick as we can be.
For phosgene and mustard gas is much too much for
   me.

They're killing us, they're killing us.
One respirator for the four of us.
Thank your lucky stars that we can all run fast.
So one of us can take it all alone.

Soldiers' song

Breakfast

We ate our breakfast lying on our backs,
Because the shells were screeching overhead.
I bet a rasher to a loaf of bread
That Hull United would beat Halifax
When Jimmy Stainthorp played full-back instead
Of Billy Bradford. Ginger raised his head
And cursed, and took the bet; and dropt back dead.
We ate our breakfast lying on our backs,
Because the shells were screeching overhead.

Wilfrid Gibson

In the Trenches

I

Not that we are weary,
Not that we fear,
Not that we are lonely
Though never alone –
Not these, not these destroy us;
But that each rush and crash
Of mortar and shell,
Each cruel bitter shriek of bullet
That tears the wind like a blade,
Each wound on the breast of earth,   10
Of Demeter, our Mother,
Wound us also,
Sever and rend the fine fabric
Of the wings of our frail souls,
Scatter into dust the bright wings
Of Psyche!

II

Impotent,
How important is all this clamour,
This destruction and contest . . .

Night after night comes the moon   20
Haughty and perfect;
Night after night the Pleiades sing
And Orion swings his belt across the sky.
Night after night the frost
Crumbles the hard earth.

Soon the spring will drop flowers
And patient creeping stalk and leaf
Along these barren lines
Where the huge rats scuttle
And the hawk shrieks to the carrion crow.   30

Can you stay them with your noise?
Then kill winter with your cannon,
Hold back Orion with your bayonets
And crush the spring leaf with your armies!

Richard Aldington

Winter Warfare

Colonel Cold strode up the Line
   (Tabs of rime and spurs of ice),
Stiffened all where he did glare,
   Horses, men, and lice.

Visited a forward post,
   Left them burning, ear to foot;
Fingers stuck to biting steel,
   Toes to frozen boot.

Stalked on into No Man's Land,
   Turned the wire to fleecy wool,   10
Iron stakes to sugar sticks
   Snapping at a pull.

Those who watched with hoary eyes
   Saw two figures gleaming there;
Hauptman Kälte, Colonel Cold,
   Gaunt, in the grey air.

Stiffly, tinkling spurs they moved
   Glassy eyed, with glinting heel
Stabbing those who lingered there
   Torn by screaming steel.   20

Edgell Rickword

Futility

Move him into the sun –
Gently its touch awoke him once,
At home, whispering of fields unsown.
Always it awoke him, even in France,
Until this morning and this snow.
If anything might rouse him now
The kind old sun will know.

Think how it wakes the seeds –
Woke, once, the clays of a cold star.
Are limbs so dear-achieved, are sides   10
Full-nerved, – still warm, – too hard to stir?
Was it for this the clay grew tall?
– O what made fatuous sunbeams toil
To break earth's sleep at all?

Wilfred Owen

Exposure

I

Our brains ache, in the merciless iced east winds that
        knife us . . .
Wearied we keep awake because the night is silent . . .
Low drooping flares confuse our memory of the
        salient . . .
Worried by silence, sentries whisper, curious, nervous,
        But nothing happens.

Watching, we hear the mad gusts tugging on the wire.
Like twitching agonies of men among its brambles.
Northward incessantly, the flickering gunnery rumbles,
Far off, like a dull rumour of some other war.
        What are we doing here?   10

The poignant misery of dawn begins to grow . . .
We only know war lasts, rain soaks, and clouds sag
        stormy.
Dawn massing in the east her melancholy army
Attacks once more in ranks on shivering ranks of gray,
        But nothing happens.

Sudden successive flights of bullets streak the silence.
Less deadly than the air that shudders black with snow,
With sidelong flowing flakes that flock, pause and
        renew,
We watch them wandering up and down the wind's
        nonchalance,
        But nothing happens.   20

Pale flakes with lingering stealth come feeling for
          our faces –
We cringe in holes, back on forgotten dreams, and
          stare, snow-dazed,
Deep into grassier ditches. So we drowse, sun-dozed,
Littered with blossoms trickling where the blackbird
          fusses.
          Is it that we are dying?

Slowly our ghosts drag home: glimpsing the sunk fires
          glozed
With crusted dark-red jewels; crickets jingle there;
For hours the innocent mice rejoice: the house is theirs;
Shutters and doors all closed: on us the doors are
          closed –
          We turn back to our dying.   30

Since we believe not otherwise can kind fires burn;
Now ever suns smile true on child, or field, or fruit.
For God's invincible spring our love is made afraid;
Therefore, not loath, we lie out here; therefore were
          born,
          For love of God seems dying.

To-night, His frost will fasten on this mud and us,
Shrivelling many hands and puckering foreheads crisp.

The burying-party, picks and shovels in their shaking
                    grasp,
Pause over half-known faces. All their eyes are ice,
          But nothing happens.   40

                                        Wilfred Owen

          'We're here because we're here'

We're here
Because
We're here
Because
We're here
Because we're here.

                                        Soldiers' song

Poem
Abbreviated from the
Conversation of Mr. T. E. H.

Over the flat slope of St. Eloi
A wide wall of sandbags.
Night,
In the silence desultory men
Pottering over small fires, cleaning their mess-tins:
To and fro, from the lines,
Men walk as on Piccadilly,
Making paths in the dark,
Through scattered dead horses,
Over a dead Belgian's belly.   10

The Germans have rockets. The English have no
    rockets.
Behind the lines, cannon, hidden, lying back miles.
Before the line, chaos:

My mind is a corridor. The minds about me are
    corridors.
Nothing suggests itself. There is nothing to do but keep
    on.

Ezra Pound

58

Illusions

Trenches in the moonlight, allayed with lulling
    moonlight
Have had their loveliness; when dancing dewy grasses
Caressed us trampling along their earthy lanes;
When the crucifix hanging over was strangely illumined,
And one imagined music, one even heard the brave bird
In the sighing orchards flute above the weedy well.
There are such moments; forgive me that I throne them,
Nor gloze that there comes soon the nemesis of beauty,
In the fluttering relics that at first glimmer awakened
Terror – the no-man's ditch suddenly forking: 10
There, the enemy's best with bombs and brains and
    courage!
– Soft, swiftly, at once be animal and angel –
But O no, no, they're Death's malkins dangling in the
    wire
    For the moon's interpretation.

Edmund Blunden

The Silent One

Who died on the wires, and hung there, one of two –
Who for his hours of life had chattered through
Infinite lovely chatter of Bucks accent:
Yet faced unbroken wires; stepped over, and went
A noble fool, faithful to his stripes – and ended.
But I weak, hungry, and willing only for the chance
Of line – to fight in the line, lay down under unbroken
Wires, and saw the flashes, and kept unshaken,
Till the politest voice – a finicking accent, said:
'Do you think you might crawl through, there;
  there's a hole'   10
Darkness, shot at: I smiled, as politely replied –
'I'm afraid not, Sir.' There was no hole no way to be seen
Nothing but chance of death, after tearing of clothes
Kept flat, and watched the darkness, hearing bullets whizzing –
And thought of music – and swore deep heart's deep oaths
(Polite to God) and retreated and came on again,
Again retreated – and a second time faced the screen.

Ivor Gurney

Moonrise over Battlefield

After the fallen sun the wind was sad
like violins behind immense old walls.
Trees were musicians swaying round the bed
of a woman in gloomy halls.

In privacy of music she made ready
with comb and silver dust and fard;
under her silken vest her little belly
shone like a bladder of sweet lard.

She drifted with the grand air of a punk
on Heaven's streets soliciting white saints;   10
then lay in bright communion on a cloud-bank
as one who near extreme of pleasure faints.

Then I thought, standing in the ruined trench,
(all around, dead Boche white-shirted lay like sheep),
'Why does this damned entrancing bitch
seek lovers only among them that sleep?'

Edgell Rickword

The Redeemer

Darkness: the rain sluiced down; the mire was deep;
It was past twelve on a mid-winter night,
When peaceful folk in beds lay snug asleep:
There, with much work to do before the light,
We lugged our clay-sucked boots as best we might
Along the trench; sometimes a bullet sang,
And droning shells burst with a hollow bang;
We were soaked, chilled and wretched, every one.
Darkness: the distant wink of a huge gun.

I turned in the black ditch, loathing the storm;   10
A rocket fizzed and burned with blanching flare,
And lit the face of what had been a form
Floundering in mirk. He stood before me there;
I say that he was Christ; stiff in the glare,
And leaning forward from his burdening task,
Both arms supporting it; his eyes on mine
Stared from the woeful head that seemed a mask
Of mortal pain in Hell's unholy shrine.

No thorny crown, only a woollen cap
He wore – an English soldier, white and strong,   20
Who loved his time like any simple chap,
Good days of work and sport and homely song;
Now he has learned that nights are very long,
And dawn a watching of the windowed sky.
But to the end, unjudging, he'll endure
Horror and pain, not uncontent to die
That Lancaster on Lune may stand secure.

He faced me, reeling in his weariness,
Shouldering his load of planks, so hard to bear.
I say that he was Christ, who wrought to bless   30
All groping things with freedom bright as air,
And with His mercy washed and made them fair.
Then the flame sank, and all grew black as pitch,
While we began to struggle along the ditch;
And someone flung his burden in the muck,
Mumbling: 'O Christ Almighty, now I'm stuck!'

Siegfried Sassoon

Serenade

It was after the Somme, our line was quieter,
Wires mended, neither side daring attacker
Or aggressor to be – the guns equal, the wires a thick
    hedge,
Where there sounded, (O past days for ever
    confounded!)
The tune of Schubert which belonged to days
    mathematical,
Effort of spirit bearing fruit worthy, actual.
The gramophone for an hour was my quiet's mocker,
Until I cried, 'Give us "Heldenleben", "Heldenleben".'
The Gloucesters cried out 'Strauss is our favourite wir
    haben
Sich geliebt'. So silence fell, Aubers front slept,   10
And the sentries an unsentimental silence kept.
True, the size of the rum ration was still a shocker
But at last over Aubers the majesty of the dawn's veil
    swept.

Ivor Gurney

Behind the Lines

Returning, We Hear The Larks

Sombre the night is:
And though we have our lives, we know
What sinister threat lurks there.

Dragging these anguished limbs, we only know
This poison-blasted track opens on our camp –
On a little safe sleep.

But hark! Joy – joy – strange joy.
Lo! Heights of night ringing with unseen larks:
Music showering our upturned listening faces.

Death could drop from the dark   10
As easily as song –
But song only dropped,
Like a blind man's dreams on the sand
By dangerous tides;
Like a girl's dark hair, for she dreams no ruin lies there,
Or her kisses where a serpent hides.

Isaac Rosenberg

After War

One got peace of heart at last, the dark march over,
And the straps slipped, the body felt under roof's low
    cover,
Lying slack the body, let sink in straw giving;
And some sweetness, a great sweetness felt in mere
    living,
And to come to this, haven after sorefooted weeks,
The dark barn roof, and the glows and the wedges and
    streaks,
Letters from home, dry warmth and still sure rest taken
Sweet to the chilled frame, nerves soothed were so sore
    shaken.

Ivor Gurney

Grotesque

These are the damned circles Dante trod,
Terrible in hopelessness,
But even skulls have their humour,
An eyeless and sardonic mockery:
And we,
Sitting with streaming eyes in the acrid smoke,
That murks our foul, damp billet,
Chant bitterly, with raucous voices
As a choir of frogs
In hideous irony, our patriotic songs. 10

Frederic Manning

Louse Hunting

Nudes, stark and glistening,
Yelling in lurid glee. Grinning faces
And raging limbs
Whirl over the floor one fire.
For a shirt verminously busy
Yon soldier tore from his throat,
With oaths
Godhead might shrink at, but not the lice,
And soon the shirt was aflare
Over the candle he'd lit while we lay.   10

Then we all sprang up and stript
To hunt the verminous brood.
Soon like a demons' pantomine
This plunge was raging.
See the silhouettes agape,
See the gibbering shadows
Mixed with the baffled arms on the wall.
See Gargantuan hooked fingers
Pluck in supreme flesh
To smutch supreme littleness.   20
See the merry limbs in that Highland fling
Because some wizard vermin willed
To charm from the quiet this revel
When our ears were half lulled
By the dark music
Blown from Sleep's trumpet.

Isaac Rosenberg

At Senlis Once

O how comely it was and how reviving
When with clay and with death no longer striving
    Down firm roads we came to houses
    With women chattering and green grass thriving.

Now though rains in a cataract descended,
We could glow, with our tribulation ended –
    Count not days, the present only
    Was thought of, how could it ever be expended?

Clad so cleanly, this remnant of poor wretches
Picked up life like the hens in orchard ditches,   10
    Gazed on the mill-sails, heard the church-bell,
    Found an honest glass all manner of riches.

How they crowded the barn with lusty laughter,
Hailed the pierrots and shook each shadowy rafter,
    Even could ridicule their own sufferings,
    Sang as though nothing but joy came after!

                            Edmund Blunden

Crucifix Corner

There was a water dump there, and regimental
Carts came every day to line up and fill full
Those rolling tanks with chlorinated clear mixture;
And curse the mud with vain veritable vexture.
Aveluy across the valley, billets, shacks, ruins,
With time and time a crump there to mark doings.
On New Year's Eve the marsh glowed tremulous
With rosy mist still holding late marvellous
Sun-glow, the air smelt home; the time breathed home.
Noel not put away; new term not yet come,   10
All things said 'Severn', the air was full of those calm
    meadows;
Transport rattled somewhere in the southern shadows;
Stars that were not strange ruled the most quiet high
Arch of soft sky, starred and most grave to see, most
    high.
What should break that but gun-noise or last Trump?
But neither came. At sudden, with light jump
Clarinet sang into 'Hundred Pipers and A'',
Aveluy's Scottish answered with pipers' true call
'Happy we've been a'together.' When nothing
Stayed of war-weariness or winter's loathing,   20
Crackers with Christmas stockings hung in the heavens,
Gladness split discipline in sixes and sevens,

Hunger ebb'd magically mixed with strange leavens;
Forgotten, forgotten the hard time's true clothing,
And stars were happy to see Man making Fate
    plaything.

Ivor Gurney

Vlamertinghe: Passing the Chateau, July, 1917

'And all her silken flanks with garlands drest' –
But we are coming to the sacrifice.
Must those have flowers who are not yet gone West?
May those have flowers who live with death and lice?
This must be the floweriest place
That earth allows; the queenly face
Of the proud mansion borrows grace for grace
Spite of those brute guns lowing at the skies.

Bold great daisies' golden lights,
Bubbling roses' pinks and whites –   10
Such a gay carpet! poppies by the million;
Such damask! such vermilion!
But if you ask me, mate, the choice of colour
Is scarcely right; this red should have been duller.

Edmund Blunden

Dead Cow Farm

An ancient saga tells us how
In the beginning the First Cow
(For nothing living yet had birth
But Elemental Cow on earth)
Began to lick cold stones and mud:
Under her warm tongue flesh and blood
Blossomed, a miracle to believe:
And so was Adam born, and Eve.
Here now is chaos once again,
Primeval mud, cold stones and rain.   10
Here flesh decays and blood drips red,
And the Cow's dead, the old Cow's dead.

Robert Graves

The Sower
(Eastern France)

Familiar, year by year, to the creaking wain
Is the long road's level ridge above the plain.
To-day a battery comes with horses and guns
On the straight road, that under the poplars runs,
At leisurely pace, the guns with mouths declined,
Harness merrily ringing, and dust behind.
Makers of widows, makers of orphans, they
Pass to their burial business, alert and gay.

But down in the field, where sun has the furrow dried,
Is a man who walks in the furrow with even stride.   10
At every step, with elbow jerked across,
He scatters seed in a quick, deliberate toss,
The immemorial gesture of Man confiding
To Earth, that restores tenfold in a season's gliding.
He is grave and patient, sowing his children's bread:
He treads the kindly furrow, nor turns his head.

Laurence Binyon

August, 1918
(In a French Village)

I hear the tinkling of the cattle bell,
In the broad stillness of the afternoon;
High in the cloudless haze the harvest moon
Is pallid as the phantom of a shell.
A girl is drawing water from a well,
I hear the clatter of her wooden shoon;
Two mothers to their sleeping babies croon;
And the hot village feels the drowsy spell.

Sleep, child, the Angel of Death his wings has spread;
His engines scour the land, the sea, the sky;   10
And all the weapons of Hell's armoury
Are ready for the blood that is their bread;
And many a thousand men to-night must die;
So many that they will not count the Dead.

Maurice Baring

'Therefore is the name of it called Babel'

And still we stood and stared far down
Into that ember-glowing town,
Which every shaft and shock of fate
Had shorn unto its base. Too late
   Came carelessly Serenity.

Now torn and broken houses gaze
On to the rat-infested maze
That once sent up rose-silver haze
   To mingle through eternity.

The outlines, once so strongly wrought,   10
Of city walls, are now a thought
Or jest unto the dead who fought . . .
   Foundation for futurity.

The shimmering sands where once there played
Children with painted pail and spade
Are drearily desolate – afraid
   To meet night's dark humanity,

Whose silver cool remakes the dead,
And lays no blame on any head
For all the havoc, fire, and lead,   20
   That fell upon us suddenly,

When all we came to know as good
Gave way to Evil's fiery flood,
And monstrous myths of iron and blood
    Seem to obscure God's clarity.

Deep sunk in sin, this tragic star
Sinks deeper still, and wages war
Against itself; strewn all the seas
With victims of a world disease
– and we are left to drink the lees   30
Of Babel's direful prophecy.

Osbert Sitwell

War

Where war has left its wake of whitened bone,
Soft stems of summer grass shall wave again,
And all the blood that war has ever strewn
                Is but a passing stain.

Lesley Coulson

Comrades of War

Canadians

We marched, and saw a company of Canadians
Their coats weighed eighty pounds at least, we saw
  them
Faces infinitely grimed in, with almost dead hands
Bent, slouching downwards to billets comfortless and
  dim.
Cave dwellers last of tribes they seemed, and a pity
Even from us just relieved (much as they were), left us.
Lord, what a land of desolation, what iniquity
Of mere being, there of what youth that country bereft
  us;
Plagues of evil lay in Death's Valley we also had
Forded that up to the thighs in chill mud   10
Gone for five days then any sign of life glow,
As the notched stumps or the gray clouds then we
  stood;
Dead past death from first hour and the needed mood
Of level pain shifting continually to and fro,
Saskatchewan, Ontario, Jack London ran in
My own mind; what in others? these men who finely
Perhaps had chosen danger for reckless and fine chance,
Fate had sent for suffering and dwelling obscenely
Vermin eaten, fed beastly, in vile ditches meanly.

Ivor Gurney

Banishment

I am banished from the patient men who fight
They smote my heart to pity, built my pride.
Shoulder to aching shoulder, side by side,
They trudged away from life's broad wealds of light.
Their wrongs were mine; and ever in my sight
They went arrayed in honour. But they died, –
Not one by one: and mutinous I cried
To those who sent them out into the night.

The darkness tells how vainly I have striven
To free them from the pit where they must dwell   10
In outcast gloom convulsed and jagged and riven
By grappling guns. Love drove me to rebel.
Love drives me back to grope with them through hell;
And in their tortured eyes I stand forgiven.

Siegfried Sassoon

Woodbine Willie

They gave me this name like their nature,
  Compacted of laughter and tears,
A sweet that was born of the bitter,
  A joke that was torn from the years.

Of their travail and torture, Christ's fools,
  Atoning my sins with their blood,
Who grinned in their agony sharing
  The glorious madness of God.

Their name! Let me hear it – the symbol
  Of unpaid-unpayable debt,   10
For the men to whom I owed God's peace,
  I put off with a cigarette.

G. A. Studdert Kennedy

Apologia pro Poemate Meo

I, too, saw God through mud –
    The mud that cracked on cheeks when wretches
      smiled.
    War brought more glory to their eyes than blood,
    And gave their laughs more glee than shakes a
      child.

Merry it was to laugh there –
    Where death becomes absurd and life absurder.
    For power was on us as we slashed bones bare
    Not to feel sickness or remorse of murder.

I, too, have dropped off fear –
    Behind the barrage, dead as my platoon,   10
    And sailed my spirit surging, light and clear
    Past the entanglement where hopes lay strewn;

And witnessed exultation –
    Faces that used to curse me, scowl for scowl,
    Shine and lift up with passion of oblation,
    Seraphic for an hour; though they were foul.

I have made fellowships –
    Untold of happy lovers in old song.
    For love is not the binding of fair lips
    With the soft silk of eyes that look and long,   20

By Joy, whose ribbon slips, –
>   But wound with war's hard wire whose stakes are
>   strong;
>   Bound with the bandage of the arm that drips;
>   Knit in the welding of the rifle-thong.

I have perceived much beauty
>   In the hoarse oaths that kept our courage straight;
>   Heard music in the silentness of duty;
>   Found peace where shell-storms spouted reddest
>   spate.

Nevertheless, except you share
>   With them in hell the sorrowful dark of hell,   30
>   Whose world is but the trembling of a flare,
>   And heaven but as the highway for a shell,

You shall not hear their mirth:
>   You shall not come to think them well content
>   By any jest of mine. These men are worth
>   Your tears: You are not worth their merriment.

Wilfred Owen

My Company

Foule! Ton âme entière est debout dans mon corps.
Jules Romains

i

You became
In many acts and quiet observances
A body and a soul, entire . . .

I cannot tell
What time your life became mine:
Perhaps when one summer night
We halted on the roadside
In the starlight only,
And you sang your sad home-songs,
Dirges which I standing outside your soul   10
Coldly condemned.

Perhaps, one night, descending cold,
When rum was mighty acceptable,
And my doling gave birth to sensual gratitude.

And then our fights: we've fought together
Compact, unanimous;
And I have felt the pride of leadership.

In many acts and quiet observances
You absorbed me:

Until one day I stood eminent 20
And I saw you gathered round me,
Uplooking,
And about you a radiance that seemed to beat
With variant glow and to give
Grace to our unity.

But, God! I know that I'll stand
Someday in the loneliest wilderness,
Someday my heart will cry
For the soul that has been, but that now
Is scattered with the winds, 30
Deceased and devoid.

I know that I'll wander with a cry:
'O beautiful men, O men I loved,
O whither are you gone, my company?'

This is a hell
Immortal while I live.

II

My men go wearily
With their monstrous burdens.

They bear wooden planks
And iron sheeting 40
Through the area of death.

When flare curves through the sky
They rest immobile.

Then on again,
Sweating and blaspheming –
'Oh, bloody Christ!'

My men, my modern Christs,
Your bloody agony confronts the world.

III

A man of mine
          lies on the wire.   50
It is death to fetch his soulless corpse.

A man of mine
          lies on the wire;
And he will rot
And first his lips
The worms will eat.

It is not thus I would have him kissed
But with the warm passionate lips
Of his comrade here.

IV – I

Kenneth Farrar is typical of many: 60
He smokes his pipe with a glad heart
And makes his days serene;
He fights hard,
And in his speech he hates the Boche: –
But really he doesn't care a damn.
His sexual experience is wide and various
And his curses are rather original.

But I've seen him kiss a dying man;
And if he comes thro' all right
(So he says)   70
He'll settle down and marry.

IV – 2

But Malyon says this:
'Old Ken's a wandering fool;
If we come thro'
Our souls will never settle in suburban hearths;
We'll linger our remaining days
Unsettled, haunted by the wrong that's done us;
The best among us will ferment
A better world;
The rest will gradually subside,   80
Unknown,
In unknown lands.'

And Ken will jeer:
'The natives of Samoa
Are suitably naïve.'

V

I can assume
A giant attitude and godlike mood,
And then detachedly regard
All riots, conflicts and collisions.

The men I've lived with   90
Lurch suddenly into a far perspective;
They distantly gather like a dark cloud of birds
In the autumn sky.

86

Urged by some unanimous
Volition or fate,
Clouds clash in opposition;
The sky quivers, the dead descend;
Earth yawns.

They are all of one species.

From my giant attitude,   100
In godlike mood,
I laugh till space is filled
with hellish merriment.

Then again I assume
My human docility,
Bow my head,
And share their doom.

Herbert Read

Before the Battle

Here on the blind verge of infinity
We live and move like moles. Our crumbling trench
Gapes like a long wound in the sodden clay.
The land is dead. No voice, no living thing,
No happy green of leaves tells that the spring
Wakes in the world behind us. Empty gloom
Fills the cold interspace of earth and sky.
The sky is waterlogged and the drenched earth
Rots, and the whining sorrow of slow shells
Flies overhead. But memory like the rose   10
Wakes and puts forth her bright and odorous blooms
And builds green hanging gardens in the heart.

Once, in another life in other places,
Where a slow river coiled through broad green spaces
And sunlight filled the long grass of the meadows
And moving water flashed from shine to shadows
Of old green-feathered willows, bent in ranks
    Along sun-speckled banks, –
Lovely remembered things now gone forever;
I saw young men run naked by the river,   20
Thirty young soliders. Where the field-path goes,
Their boots and shirts and khaki lay in rows.

With feet among the long warm grass stood one
    Like ivory in the sun,
And in the water, white upon the shade
    That hung beneath the shore,
His long reflection like a slow flag swayed

And at a trembling of the water frayed
Into a hundred shreds, then joined once more.
One, where the river, when the willows end,   30
Breaks from its calm to swirl about a bend,
Strong swimmer he, wrestled against the race
Of the full stream. I saw his laughing face
Framed by his upcurved arm. Another, slim,
Hands above head, stood braced upon the brim,
Then dived, a brother of the curved new moon,
    And came up streaming soon
Ten feet beyond, brown shoulders shining wet
And comic face and hair washed sleet as jet.
Out on the further bank another fellow   40
Climbed stealthily into a leaning willow,
And perched leaf-shrouded, crooning like a dove,
Till from the pool below a voice was heard:
"Ere, Bert! Where's Bert?' And Bert sang out above:
'Up 'ere, old son, changed to a bloody bird!'
And dived through leaves and shattered through the
    cool
Clear watery mirror; and all across the pool
Slow winking circles opened wide, till he
Rose and in rising broke their symmetry.

Laughter and shouting filled the sparkling air.   50
Bright flakes of scattered water everywhere
Leapt from their diving. Hosts of little billows
Beat the shores, and hanging boughs of willows
Glittered with glassy drops. Then, bright as fire,
A bugle sounded, and their happy din
Stopped, and the boys, with that swift discipline
By which keen life answers the soul's desire,

Rushed for the bank. And soon the bank was bright
With bodies swarming up out of the stream.
From the water and the boughs they came in sight: 60
Across the leaves I saw their quick limbs gleam.
Then brandished towels flashed whitely here and there.
They dried their ears and scrubbed their towzled hair.
One, stepping to the water, carefully
Stretched a bare leg to rinse a muddy foot:
    One sat with updrawn knee,
Bent head, and both hands tugging on a boot.
And gradually the bright and flashing crowd
Dimmed into sober khaki. Then the loud
Laughter and shouts and songs died at a word.   70
The ranks fell in: No sound, no movement stirred.
The willow-boughs were still: the blue sky burned:
The party numbered down, formed fours, right turned,
Marched. And their shadows faded from the stream
And the dark pool swayed back into its dream:
Only the trodden meadow-grass reported
Where all that gay humanity had sported.

So the dream fades. I wake, remembering how
Many of those smart boys no longer now
Cast running shadows on the grass or make   80
    White tents with laughter shake,
But lie in narrow chambers underground,
Eyes void of sunlight, ears unthrilled by sound
Of laughter. Round my post on every hand
Stretches this grim, charred skeleton of land
Where ruined homes and shell-ploughed fields are lost
In one great sea of clay, clay seared by fire,
Battered by rainstorms, jagged and scarred and crossed

By gaping trench-lines hedged with rusted wire.
The rainy evening fades. A rainy night
Sags down upon us. Wastes of sodden clay
Fade into mist, and fade all sound and sight,
All broken sounds and movements of the day,
To emptiness and listlessness, a grey
Unhappy silence tremulous with the poise
Of hearts intent with fearful expectation
    And secret preparation,
Silence that is not peace but bated breath,
    A listening for death,
    The quivering prelude to tremendous noise.

O give us one more day of sun and leaves,
The laughing soldiers and the laughing stream,
And when at dawn the loud destruction cleaves
The silence, and (like men that walk in dream,
Knowing the stern ordeal has begun)
We climb the trench, and cross the wire and start,
We'll stumble through the shell-bursts with good heart
Like boys who race through meadows in the sun.

Martin Armstrong

Nameless Men

Around me, when I wake or sleep,
Men strange to me their vigils keep;
And some were boys but yesterday,
Upon the village green at play.
Their faces I shall never know;
Like sentinels they come and go.
In grateful love I bow the knee
For nameless men who die for me.

There is in earth or heaven no room
Where I may flee this dreadful doom.　　　　10
For ever it is understood
I am a man redeemed by blood.
I must walk softly all my days
Down on my redeemed and solemn ways.
Christ, take the men I bring to Thee,
The men who watch and die for me.

Edward Shillito

Greater Love

Red lips are not so red
  As the stained stones kissed by the English dead.
Kindness of wooed and wooer
Seems shame to their love pure.
O Love, your eyes lose lure
  When I behold eyes blinded in my stead!

Your slender attitude
  Trembles not exquisite like limbs knife-skewed,
Rolling and rolling there
Where God seems not to care;
Till the fierce Love they bear
  Cramps them in death's extreme decrepitude.

Your voice sings not so soft, –
  Though even as wind murmuring through
      raftered loft, –
Your dear voice is not dear,
Gentle, and evening clear,
As theirs whom none now hear
  Now earth has stopped their piteous mouths that
      coughed.

Heart, you were never hot,
   Nor large, nor full like hearts made great
      with shot; 20
And though your hand be pale,
Paler are all which trail
Your cross through flame and hail:
   Weep, you may weep, for you may touch them not.

Wilfred Owen

In Memoriam Private D. Sutherland killed in Action in the German Trench, May 16, 1916, and the Others who Died

So you were David's father,
And he was your only son,
And the new-cut peats are rotting
And the work is left undone,
Because of an old man weeping,
Just an old man in pain,
For David, his son David,
That will not come again.

Oh, the letters he wrote you,
And I can see them still,   10
Not a word of the fighting
But just the sheep on the hill
And how you should get the crops in
Ere the year got stormier,
And the Bosches have got his body,
And I was his officer.

You were only David's father,
But I had fifty sons
When we went up in the evening
Under the arch of the guns,   20
And we came back at twilight –
O God! I heard them call
To me for help and pity
That could not help at all.

Oh, never will I forget you,
My men that trusted me,
More my sons than your fathers',
For they could only see
The little helpless babies
And the young men in their pride. 30
They could not see you dying,
And hold you while you died.

Happy and young and gallant,
They saw their first-born go,
But not the strong limbs broken
And the beautiful men brought low,
The piteous writhing bodies,
They screamed, 'Don't leave me, Sir,'
For they were only your fathers
But I was your officer. 40

E. A. Mackintosh

To his Love

He's gone, and all our plans
   Are useless indeed.
We'll walk no more on Cotswold
   Where the sheep feed
   Quietly and take no heed.

His body that was so quick
   Is not as you
Knew it, on Severn river
   Under the blue
   Driving our small boat through.   10

You would not know him now . . .
   But still he died
Nobly, so cover him over
   With violets of pride
   Purple from Severn side.

Cover him, cover him soon!
   And with thick-set
Masses of memoried flowers –
   Hide that red wet
   Thing I must somehow forget.   20

Ivor Gurney

Trench Poets

I knew a man, he was my chum,
But he grew blacker every day,
And would not brush the flies away,
Nor blanch however fierce the hum
Of passing shells; I used to read,
To rouse him, random things from Donne;
Like 'Get with child a mandrake-root,'
But you can tell he was far gone,
For he lay gaping, mackerel-eyed,
And stiff, and senseless as a post   10
Even when that old poet cried
'I long to talk with some old lover's ghost.'

I tried the Elegies one day,
But he, because he heard me say
'What needst thou have more covering than a man?'
Grinned nastily, and so I knew
The worms had got his brains at last.
There was one thing that I might do
To starve the worms; I racked my head
For healthy things and quoted '*Maud.*'   20
His grin got worse and I could see
He sneered at passion's purity.
He stank so badly, though we were great chums
I had to leave him; then rats ate his thumbs.

Edgell Rickword

3 ACTION

Rendezvous with Death

Before Action

By all the glories of the day,
　　And the cool evening's benison,
By the last sunset touch that lay
　　Upon the hills when day was done,
By beauty lavishly outpoured
　　And blessings carelessly received,
By all the days that I have lived
　　Make me a soldier, Lord.

By all of all man's hopes and fears,
　　And all the wonders poets sing,　　　　　　　　10
The laughter of unclouded years,
　　And every sad and lovely thing;
By the romantic ages stored
　　With high endeavour that was his,
By all his mad catastrophes
　　Make me a man, O Lord.

I, that on my familiar hill
　　Saw with uncomprehending eyes
A hundred of Thy sunsets spill
　　Their fresh and sanguine sacrifice,　　　　　　20
Ere the sun swings his noonday sword

Must say good-bye to all of this; –
By all delights that I shall miss,
    Help me to die, O Lord.

W. N. *Hodgson*

Into Battle

The naked earth is warm with Spring,
    And with green grass and bursting trees
Leans to the sun's gaze glorying,
    And quivers in the sunny breeze;
And Life is Colour and Warmth and Light,
    And a striving evermore for these;
And he is dead who will not fight;
    And who dies fighting has increase.

The fighting man shall from the sun
    Take warmth, and life from the glowing earth;   10
Speed with the light-foot winds to run,
    And with the trees to newer birth;
And find, when fighting shall be done,
    Great rest, and fullness after dearth.

All the bright company of Heaven
    Hold him in their high comradeship,
The Dog-Star, and the Sisters Seven,
    Orion's Belt and sworded hip.

The woodland trees that stand together,
    They stand to him each one a friend;   20
They gently speak in the windy weather;
    They guide to valley and ridge's end.

The kestrel hovering by day,
    And the little owls that call by night,
Bid him be swift and keen as they,
    As keen of ear, as swift of sight.

The blackbird sings to him, 'Brother, brother,
    If this be the last song you shall sing,
Sing well, for you may not sing another;
    Brother, sing.'   30

In dreary doubtful waiting hours,
    Before the brazen frenzy starts,
The horses show him nobler powers;
    O patient eyes, courageous hearts!

And when the burning moment breaks,
    And all things else are out of mind,
And only Joy-of-Battle takes
    Him by the throat, and makes him blind,

Through joy and blindness he shall know,
    Not caring much to know, that still   40
Nor lead nor steel shall reach him, so
    That it be not the Destined Will.

The thundering line of battle stands,
    And in the air Death moans and sings:
But Day shall clasp him with strong hands,
    And Night shall fold him in soft wings.

Julian Grenfell

Lights Out

I have come to the borders of sleep,
The unfathomable deep
Forest where all must lose
Their way, however straight,
Or winding, soon or late;
They cannot choose.

Many a road and track
That, since the dawn's first crack,
Up to the forest brink,
Deceived the travellers,   10
Suddenly now blurs,
And in they sink.

Here love ends,
Despair, ambition ends,
All pleasure and all trouble,
Although most sweet or bitter,
Here ends in sleep that is sweeter
Than tasks most noble.

There is not any book
Or face of dearest look   20
That I would not turn from now
To go into the unknown
I must enter and leave alone
I know not how.

The tall forest towers;
Its cloudy foliage lowers
Ahead, shelf above shelf;
Its silence I hear and obey
That I may lose my way
And myself.   30

                                        Edward Thomas

'I have a rendezvous with Death'

I have a rendezvous with Death
At some disputed barricade,
When Spring comes back with rustling shade
And apple-blossoms fill the air –
I have a rendezvous with Death
When Spring brings back blue days and fair.

It may be he shall take my hand
And lead me into his dark land
And close my eyes and quench my breath –
It may be I shall pass him still.   10
I have a rendezvous with Death
On some scarred slope of battered hill,
When Spring comes round again this year
And the first meadow-flowers appear.

God knows 'twere better to be deep
Pillowed in silk and scented down,
Where Love throbs out in blissful sleep,
Pulse nigh to pulse, and breath to breath,
Where hushed awakenings are dear . . .
But I've a rendezvous with Death   20
At midnight in some flaming town,
When Spring trips north again this year,
And I to my pledged word am true,
I shall not fail that rendezvous.

Alan Seeger

Two Sonnets

I

Saints have adored the lofty soul of you.
Poets have whitened at your high renown.
We stand among the many millions who
Do hourly wait to pass your pathway down.
You, so familiar, once were strange: we tried
To live as of your presence unaware.
But now in every road on every side
We see your straight and steadfast signpost there.

I think it like that signpost in my land,
Hoary and tall, which pointed me to go   10
Upward, into the hills, on the right hand,
Where the mists swim and the winds shriek and blow,
A homeless land and friendless, but a land
I did not know and that I wished to know.

II

Such, such is Death: no triumph: no defeat:
Only an empty pail, a slate rubbed clean,
A merciful putting away what has been.

And this we know: Death is not Life effete,
Life crushed, the broken pail. We who have seen
So marvellous things know well the end not yet.

Victor and vanquished are a-one in death:
Coward and brave: friend, foe. Ghosts do not say
'Come, what was your record when you drew breath?'

But a big blot has hid each yesterday
So poor, so manifestly incomplete.
And your bright Promise, withered long and sped,
Is touched, stirs, rises, opens and grows sweet
And blossoms and is you, when you are dead.

Charles Hamilton Sorley

1914: The Soldier

If I should die, think only this of me:
  That there's some corner of a foreign field
That is for ever England. There shall be
  In that rich earth a richer dust concealed;
A dust whom England bore, shaped, made aware,
  Gave, once, her flowers to love, her ways to roam,
A body of England's, breathing English air,
  Washed by the rivers, blest by suns of home.

And think, this heart, all evil shed away,
  A pulse in the eternal mind, no less   10
    Gives somewhere back the thoughts by England
      given;
Her sights and sounds; dreams happy as her day;
  And laughter, learnt of friends; and gentleness,
    In hearts at peace, under an English heaven.

Rupert Brooke

The Mother
Written after reading Rupert Brooke's sonnet,
'The Soldier'

If you should die, think only this of me
In that still quietness where is space for thought,
Where parting, loss and bloodshed shall not be,
And men may rest themselves and dream of nought:
That in some place a mystic mile away
One whom you loved has drained the bitter cup
Till there is nought to drink; has faced the day
Once more, and now, has raised the standard up.

And think, my son, with eyes grown clear and dry
She lives as though for ever in your sight,   10
Loving the things *you* loved, with heart aglow
For country, honour, truth, traditions high,
– Proud that you paid their price. (And if some night
Her heart should break – well, lad, you will not know.)

May Herschel-Clark

'I tracked a dead man down a trench'

I tracked a dead man down a trench,
    I knew not he was dead.
They told me he had gone that way,
    And there his foot-marks led.

The trench was long and close and curved,
    It seemed without an end;
And as I threaded each new bay
    I thought to see my friend.

I went there stooping to the ground.
    For, should I raise my head,   10
Death watched to spring; and how should then
    A dead man find the dead?

At last I saw his back. He crouched
    As still as still could be,
And when I called his name aloud
    He did not answer me.

The floor-way of the trench was wet
    Where he was crouching dead:
The water of the pool was brown,
    And round him it was red.   20

I stole up softly where he stayed
    With head hung down all slack,
And on his shoulders laid my hands
    And drew him gently back.

And then, as I had guessed, I saw
   His head, and how the crown –
I saw then why he crouched so still,
   And why his head hung down.

W. S. S. Lyon

Ballad of the Three Spectres

As I went up by Ovillers
    In mud and water cold to the knee,
There went three jeering, fleering spectres,
    That walked abreast and talked of me.

The first said, 'Here's a right brave soldier
    That walks the dark unfearingly;
Soon he'll come back on a fine stretcher,
    And laughing for a nice Blighty.'

The second, 'Read his face, old comrade,
    No kind of lucky chance I see;   10
One day he'll freeze in mud to the marrow,
    Then look his last on Picardie.'

Though bitter the word of these first twain
    Curses the third spat venomously;
'He'll stay untouched till the war's last dawning
    Then live one hour of agony.'

Liars the first two were. Behold me
    At sloping arms by one – two – three;
Waiting the time I shall discover
    Whether the third spake verity.   20

Ivor Gurney

The Question

I wonder if the old cow died or not?
    Gey bad she was the night I left, and sick.
Dick reckoned she would mend. He knows a lot –
    At least he fancies so himself, does Dick.

Dick knows a lot. But happen I did wrong
    To leave the cow to him and come away.
Over and over like a silly song
    These words keep bumming in my head all day.

And all I think of, as I face the foe
    And take my lucky chance of being shot,   10
Is this – that if I'm hit, I'll never know
    Till Doomsday if the old cow died or not.

Wilfrid Gibson

The Soldier Addresses His Body

I shall be mad if you get smashed about;
We've had good times together, you and I;
Although you groused a bit when luck was out,
And women passionless, and we went dry.

Yet there are many things we have not done;
Countries not seen, where people do strange things;
Eat fish alive, and mimic in the sun
The solemn gestures of their stone-grey kings.

I've heard of forests that are dim at noon
Where snakes and creepers wrestle all day long;   10
Where vivid beasts grow pale with the full moon,
Gibber and cry, and wail a mad old song;

Because at the full moon the Hippogriff,
With crinkled ivory snout and agate feet,
With his green eyes will glare them cold and stiff
For the coward Wyvern to come down and eat.

Vodka and kvass, and bitter mountain wines
We have not drunk, nor snatched at bursting grapes
To pelt slim girls along Sicilian vines
Who'd flicker through the leaves, faint frolic shapes.   20

Yea, there are many things we have not done,
But it's a sweat to knock them into rhyme,
Let's have a drink, and give the cards a run
And leave dull verse to the dull peaceful time.

Edgell Rickword

The Day's March

The battery grides and jingles,
Mile succeeds to mile;
Shaking the noonday sunshine
The guns lunge out awhile,
And then are still awhile.

We amble along the highway;
The reeking, powdery dust
Ascends and cakes our faces
With a striped, sweaty crust.

Under the still sky's violet   10
The heat throbs on the air . . .
The white road's dusty radiance
Assumes a dark glare.

With a head hot and heavy,
And eyes that cannot rest,
And a black heart burning
In a stifled breast,

I sit in the saddle,
I feel the road unroll,
And keep my senses straightened   20
Toward to-morrow's goal.

There, over unknown meadows
Which we must reach at last,

Day and night thunders
A black and chilly blast.

Heads forget heaviness,
Hearts forget spleen,
For by that mighty winnowing
Being is blown clean.

Light in the eyes again,   30
Strength in the hand,
A spirit dares, dies, forgives,
And can understand!

And, best! Love comes back again
After grief and shame,
And along the wind of death
Throws a clean flame.

                              *

The battery grides and jingles,
Mile succeeds to mile;
Suddenly battering the silence   40
The guns burst out awhile.

                              *

I lift my head and smile.

                                        Robert Nichols

Battle

Eve of Assault: Infantry Going Down to Trenches

Downwards slopes the wild red sun.
We lie around a waiting gun;
Soon we shall load and fire and load.
But, hark! a sound beats down the road.

''Ello! wot's up?' 'Let's 'ave a look!'
'Come on, Ginger, drop that book!'
'Wot an 'ell of bloody noise!'
'It's the Yorks and Lancs, meboys!'

So we crowd: watch them come –
One man drubbing on a drum,   10
A crazy, high mouth-organ blowing,
Tin cans rattling, cat-calls, crowing . . .

And above their rhythmic feet
A whirl of shrilling loud and sweet,
Round mouths whistling in unison;
Shouts: ''O's goin' to out the 'Un?'

'Back us up, mates!' 'Gawd, we will!'
''Eave them shells at Kaiser Bill!'
'Art from Lancashire, melad?'
'Gi' 'en a cheer, boys; make'en glad.'   20

''Ip 'urrah!' 'Give Fritz the chuck.'
'Good ol' bloody Yorks!' 'Good-luck!'
'Cheer!'

     I cannot cheer or speak
Lest my voice, my heart must break.

Robert Nichols

Headquarters

A league and a league from the trenches – from the
    traversed maze of the lines,
Where daylong the sniper watches and daylong the
    bullet whines,
And the cratered earth is in travail with mines and with
    countermines –

Here, where haply some woman dreamed, (are those
    her roses that bloom
In the garden beyond the windows of my littered
    working room?)
We have decked the map for our masters as a bride is
    decked for the groom.

Fair, on each lettered numbered square – cross-road and
    mound and wire,
Loophole, redoubt, and emplacement – lie the targets
    their mouths desire;
Gay with purples and browns and blues, have we
    traced them their arcs of fire.

And ever the type-keys chatter; and ever our
    keen wires bring   10
Word from the watchers a-crouch below, word from the
    watchers a-wing:
And ever we hear the distant growl of our hid guns
    thundering.

Hear it hardly, and turn again to our maps, where the
    trench-lines crawl,
Red on the gray and each with a sign for the ranging
    shrapnel's fall –
Snakes that our masters shall scotch at dawn, as is
    written here on the wall.

For the weeks of our waiting draw to a close . . . There
    is scarcely a leaf astir
In the garden beyond my windows, where the twilight
    shadows blurr
The blaze of some woman's roses . . .
                                    'Bombardment orders, sir.'

Gilbert Frankau

Bombardment

The Town has opened to the sun.
Like a flat red lily with a million petals
She unfolds, she comes undone.

A sharp sky brushes upon
The myriad glittering chimney-tips
As she gently exhales to the sun.

Hurrying creatures run
Down the labyrinth of the sinister flower.
What is it they shun?

A dark bird falls from the sun.   10
It curves in a rush to the heart of the vast
Flower: the day has begun.

D. H. Lawrence

The Shell

Shrieking its message the flying death
   Cursed the resisting air,
Then buried its nose by a battered church,
   A skeleton gaunt and bare.

The brains of science, the money of fools
   Had fashioned an iron slave
Destined to kill, yet the futile end
   Was a child's uprooted grave.

H. Smalley Sarson

Bombardment

Four days the earth was rent and torn
By bursting steel,
The houses fell about us;
Three nights we dared not sleep,
Sweating, and listening for the imminent crash
Which meant our death.

The fourth night every man,
Nerve-tortured, racked to exhaustion,
Slept, muttering and twitching,
While the shells crashed overhead.   10

The fifth day there came a hush;
We left our holes
And looked above the wreckage of the earth
To where the white clouds moved in silent lines
Across the untroubled blue.

Richard Aldington

On Somme

Suddenly into the still air burst thudding
And thudding, and cold fear possessed me all,
On the grey slopes there, where winter in sullen
    brooding
Hung between height and depth of the ugly fall
Of Heaven to earth; and the thudding was illness' own.
But still a hope I kept that were we there going over,
I, in the line, I should not fail, but take recover
From others' courage, and not as coward be known.
No flame we saw, the noise and the dread alone
Was battle to us; men were enduring there such   10
And such things, in wire tangled, to shatters blown.

Courage kept, but ready to vanish at first touch.
Fear, but just held. Poets were luckier once
In the hot fray swallowed and some magnificence.

Ivor Gurney

Before the Charge

The night is still and the air is keen,
  Tense with menace the time crawls by,
In front is the town and its homes are seen,
  Blurred in outline against the sky.

The dead leaves float in the sighing air,
  The darkness moves like a curtain drawn,
A veil which the morning sun will tear
  From the face of death. – We charge at dawn.

Patrick MacGill

It's a Queer Time

It's hard to know if you're alive or dead
When steel and fire go roaring through your head.

One moment you'll be crouching at your gun
Traversing, mowing heaps down half in fun:
The next, you choke and clutch at your right breast –
No time to think – leave all – and off you go . . .
To Treasure Island where the Spice winds blow,
To lovely groves of mango, quince and lime –
Breathe no goodbye, but ho, for the Red West!
          It's a queer time.   10

You're charging madly at them yelling 'Fag!'
When somehow something gives and your feet drag.
You fall and strike your head; yet feel no pain
And find . . . You're digging tunnels through the hay
In the Big Barn, 'cause it's a rainy day.
Oh springy hay, and lovely beams to climb!
You're back in the old sailor suit again.
          It's a queer time.

Or you'll be dozing safe in your dug-out –
A great roar – the trench shakes and falls about –   20
You're struggling, gasping, struggling, then . . . hullo!
Elsie comes tripping gaily down the trench,
Hanky to nose – that lyddite makes a stench –

Getting her pinafore all over grime.
Funny! because she died ten years ago!
     It's a queer time.

The trouble is, things happen much too quick;
Up jump the Bosches, rifles thump and click,
You stagger, and the whole scene fades away:
Even good Christians don't like passing straight   30
From Tipperary or their Hymn of Hate
To Alleluiah-chanting, and the chime
Of golden harps . . . and . . . I'm not well today . . .
     It's a queer time.

Robert Graves

The Face

Out of the smoke of men's wrath,
The red mist of anger,
Suddenly,
As a wraith of sleep,
A boy's face, white and tense,
Convulsed with terror and hate,
The lips trembling . . .

Then a red smear, falling . . .
I thrust aside the cloud, as it were tangible,
Blinded with a mist of blood.   10
The face cometh again
As a wraith of sleep:
A boy's face delicate and blonde,
The very mask of God,
Broken.

Frederic Manning

Gethsemane

The Garden called Gethsemane
  In Picardy it was,
And there the people came to see
  The English soldiers pass.
We used to pass – we used to pass
  Or halt, as it might be,
And ship our masks in case of gas
  Beyond Gethsemane.

The Garden called Gethsemane,
  It held a pretty lass,   10
But all the time she talked to me
  I prayed my cup might pass.
The officer sat on the chair,
  The men lay on the grass,
And all the time we halted there
  I prayed my cup might pass –

It didn't pass – it didn't pass –
  It didn't pass from me.
I drank it when we met the gas
  Beyond Gethsemane.   20

Rudyard Kipling

Anthem for Doomed Youth

What passing-bells for these who die as cattle?
    Only the monstrous anger of the guns.
    Only the stuttering rifles' rapid rattle
Can patter out their hasty orisons.
No mockeries for them; no prayers nor bells,
Nor any voice of mourning save the choirs, –
The shrill, demented choirs of wailing shells;
And bugles calling for them from sad shires.

What candles may be held to speed them all?
    Not in the hands of boys, but in their eyes   10
Shall shine the holy glimmers of goodbyes.
    The pallor of girls' brows shall be their pall;
Their flowers the tenderness of patient minds,
And each slow dusk a drawing-down of blinds.

Wilfred Owen

The Navigators

I saw the bodies of earth's men
    Like wharves thrust in the stream of time
    Whereon cramped navigators climb
And free themselves in the warm sun:

With outflung arms and shouts of joy
    Those spirits tramped their human planks;
    Then pressing close, reforming ranks,
They pushed off in the stream again:

Cold darkly rotting lay the wharves,
    Decaying in the stream of time;   10
    Slow winding silver tracks of slime
Showed bright where came back none.

W. J. Turner

Spring Offensive

Halted against the shade of a last hill,
They fed, and, lying easy, were at ease
And, finding comfortable chests and knees
Carelessly slept. But many there stood still
To face the stark, blank sky beyond the ridge,
Knowing their feet had come to the end of the world.

Marvelling they stood, and watched the long grass
    swirled
By the May breeze, murmurous with wasp and midge,
For though the summer oozed into their veins
Like the injected drug for their bones' pains,   10
Sharp on their souls hung the imminent line of grass,
Fearfully flashed the sky's mysterious glass.

Hour after hour they ponder the warm field –
And the far valley behind, where the buttercups
Had blessed with gold their slow boots coming up,
Where even the little brambles would not yield,
But clutched and clung to them like sorrowing hands;
They breathe like trees unstirred.

Till like a cold gust thrilled the little word
At which each body and its soul begird   20
And tighten them for battle. No alarms
Of bugles, no high flags, no clamorous haste –
Only a lift and flare of eyes that faced

The sun, like a friend with whom their love is done.
O larger shone that smile against the sun, –
Mightier than his whose bounty these have spurned.

So, soon they topped the hill, and raced together
Over an open stretch of herb and heather
Exposed. And instantly the whole sky burned
With fury against them; and soft sudden cups   30
Opened in thousands for their blood; and the green
    slopes
Chasmed and steepened sheer to infinite space.

Of them who running on that last high place
Leapt to swift unseen bullets, or went up
On the hot blast and fury of hell's upsurge,
Or plunged and fell away past this world's verge,
Some say God caught them even before they fell.

But what say such as from existence' brink
Ventured but drave too swift to sink.
The few who rushed in the body to enter hell,   40
And there out-fiending all its fiends and flames
With superhuman inhumanities,
Long-famous glories, immemorial shames –
And crawling slowly back, have by degrees
Regained cool peaceful air in wonder –
Why speak they not of comrades that went under?

                                        Wilfred Owen

Counter-Attack

We'd gained our first objective hours before
While dawn broke like a face with blinking eyes,
Pallid, unshaved and thirsty, blind with smoke.
Things seemed all right at first. We held their line,
With bombers posted, Lewis guns well placed,
And clink of shovels deepening the shallow trench.
    The place was rotten with dead; green clumsy legs
    High-booted, sprawled and grovelled along the saps;
    And trunks, face downward, in the sucking mud,
    Wallowed like trodden sand-bags loosely filled;   10
    And naked sodden buttocks, mats of hair,
    Bulged, clotted heads slept in the plastering slime.
    And then the rain began, – the jolly old rain!

A yawning soldier knelt against the bank,
Staring across the morning blear with fog;
He wondered when the Allemands would get busy;
And then, of course, they started with five-nines
Traversing, sure as fate, and never a dud.
Mute in the clamour of shells he watched them burst
Spouting dark earth and wire with gusts from hell,   20
While posturing giants dissolved in drifts of smoke.
He crouched and flinched, dizzy with galloping fear,
Sick for escape, – loathing the strangled horror
And butchered, frantic gestures of the dead.

An officer came blundering down the trench:
'Stand-to and man the fire-step!' On he went . . .
Gasping and bawling, 'Fire-step . . . counter-attack!'

Then the haze lifted. Bombing on the right
Down the old sap: machine-guns on the left;
And stumbling figures looming out in front.   30
    'O Christ, they're coming at us!' Bullets spat,
And he remembered his rifle . . . rapid fire . . .
And started blazing wildly . . . then a bang
Crumpled and spun him sideways, knocked him out
To grunt and wriggle: none heeded him; he choked
And fought the flapping veils of smothering gloom,
Lost in a blurred confusion of yells and groans . . .
Down, and down, and down, he sank and drowned,
Bleeding to death. The counter-attack had failed.

                                    Siegfried Sassoon

Youth in Arms III: Retreat

That is not war – oh it hurts! I am lame.
A thorn is burning me.
We are going back to the place from which we came.
I remember the old song now: –

> *Soldier, soldier, going to war,*
> *When will you come back?*

Mind that rut. It is very deep.
All these ways are parched and raw.
Where are we going? How we creep!
Are you there? I never saw –   10

Damn this jingle in my brain.
I'm full of old songs – Have you ever heard this?

> *All the roads to victory*
> *Are flooded as we go.*
> *There's so much blood to paddle through,*
> *That's why we're marching slow.*

Yes sir; I'm here. Are you an officer?
I can't see. Are we running away?
How long have we done it? One whole year,
A month, a week, or since yesterday?   20

Damn the jingle! My brain
Is scragged and banged –

Fellows, these are happy times;
Tramp and tramp with open eyes.
Yet, try however much you will,
You cannot see a tree, a hill,
Moon, stars or even skies.

I won't be quiet. Sing too, you fool.
I had a dog I used to beat.
Don't try it on me. Say that again.   30
Who said it? *Halt!* Why? Who can halt?
We're marching now. Who fired? Well. Well.
I'll lie down too. I'm tired enough.

Harold Monro

Aftermath

Back to Rest

A leaping wind from England,
   The skies without a stain,
Clean cut against the morning
   Slim poplars after rain,
The foolish noise of sparrows
   And starlings in a wood –
After the grime of battle
   We know that these are good.

Death whining down from Heaven,
   Death roaring from the ground,   10
Death stinking in the nostril,
   Death shrill in every sound,
Doubting we charged and conquered –
   Hopeless we struck and stood.
Now when the fight is ended
   We know that it was good.

We that have seen the strongest
   Cry like a beaten child,
The sanest eyes unholy,
   The cleanest hands defiled,   20
We that have known the heart blood

Less than the lees of wine,
We that have seen men broken,
We know man is divine.

W. N. Hodgson

Dulce et Decorum est

Bent double, like old beggars under sacks,
Knock-kneed, coughing like hags, we cursed through
    sludge,
Till on the haunting flares we turned our backs,
And towards our distant rest began to trudge.
Men marched asleep. Many had lost their boots,
But limped on, blood-shod. All went lame, all blind;
Drunk with fatigue; deaf even to the hoots
Of gas-shells dropping softly behind.

Gas! GAS! Quick, boys! – An ecstasy of fumbling
Fitting the clumsy helmets just in time,   10
But someone still was yelling out and stumbling
And flound'ring like a man in fire or lime. –
Dim through the misty panes and thick green light,
As under a green sea, I saw him drowning.

In all my dreams before my helpless sight
He plunges at me, guttering, choking, drowning.

If in some smothering dreams, you too could pace
Behind the wagon that we flung him in,
And watch the white eyes writhing in his face,
His hanging face, like a devil's sick of sin,   20
If you could hear, at every jolt, the blood
Come gargling from the froth-corrupted lungs
Bitten as the cud
Of vile, incurable sores on innocent tongues, –
My friend, you would not tell with such high zest

To children ardent for some desperate glory,
The old Lie: *Dulce et decorum est*
Pro patria mori.

Wilfred Owen

Field Ambulance in Retreat
Via Dolorosa, Via Sacra

I

A straight flagged road, laid on the rough earth,
A causeway of stone from beautiful city to city,
Between the tall trees, the slender, delicate trees,
Through the flat green land, by plots of flowers, by
  black canals thick with heat.

II

The road-makers made it well
Of fine stone, strong for the feet of the oxen and the
  great Flemish horses,
And for the high wagons piled with corn from the
  harvest.
And the labourers are few;
They and their quiet oxen stand aside and wait
By the long road loud with the passing of guns, the
  rush of armoured cars, and the tramp of an army on
  the march forward to battle;   10
And, where the piled corn-wagons went, our dripping
  Ambulance carries home
Its red and white harvest from the fields.

III

The straight flagged road breaks into dust, into a thin
  white cloud,
About the feet of a regiment driven back league by
  league,
Rifles at trail, and standards wrapped in black funeral

cloths. Unhasting, proud in retreat,
They smile as the Red Cross Ambulance rushes by.
(You know nothing of beauty and desolation who have
    not seen
That smile of an army in retreat.)
They go: and our shining, beckoning danger goes with
    them,
And our joy in the harvests that we gathered in at
    nightfall in the fields;   20
And like an unloved hand laid on a beating heart
Our safety wears us down.
Safety hard and strange; stranger and yet more hard,
As, league after dying league, the beautiful, desolate
    Land
Falls back from the intolerable speed of an Ambulance
    in retreat
On the sacred, dolorous Way.

May Sinclair

A Memory

There was no sound at all, no crying in the village,
    Nothing you would count as sound, that is, after the
      shells;
Only behind a wall the slow sobbing of women,
    The creaking of a door, a lost dog – nothing else.

Silence which might be felt, no pity in the silence,
    Horrible, soft like blood, down all the blood-stained
      ways;
In the middle of the street two corpses lie unburied,
    And a bayoneted woman stares in the market-place.

Humble and ruined folk – for these no pride of
      conquest,
    Their only prayer: 'O! Lord, give us our daily
      bread!' 10
Not by the battle fires, the shrapnel are we haunted;
    Who shall deliver us from the memory of these
      dead?

Margaret Sackville

Dead Man's Dump

The plunging limbers over the shattered track
Racketed with their rusty freight,
Stuck out like many crowns of thorns,
And the rusty stakes like sceptres old
To stay the flood of brutish men
Upon our brothers dear.

The wheels lurched over sprawled dead
But pained them not, though their bones crunched;
Their shut mouths made no moan.
They lie there huddled, friend and foeman,   10
Man born of man, and born of woman;
And shells go crying over them
From night till night and now.

Earth has waited for them,
All the time of their growth
Fretting for their decay:
Now she has them at last!
In the strength of their strength
Suspended – stopped and held.

What fierce imaginings their dark souls lit?   20
Earth! Have they gone into you?
Somewhere they must have gone,
And flung on your hard back
Is their soul's sack,
Emptied of God-ancestralled essences.
Who hurled them out? Who hurled?

None saw their spirits' shadow shake the grass,
Or stood aside for the half used life to pass
Out of those doomed nostrils and the doomed mouth,
When the swift iron burning bee   30
Drained the wild honey of their youth.

What of us who, flung on the shrieking pyre,
Walk, our usual thoughts untouched,
Our lucky limbs as on ichor fed,
Immortal seeming ever?
Perhaps when the flames beat loud on us,
A fear may choke in our veins
And the startled blood may stop.

The air is loud with death,
The dark air spurts with fire,   40
The explosions ceaseless are.
Timelessly now, some minutes past,
These dead strode time with vigorous life,
Till the shrapnel called 'An end!'
But not to all. In bleeding pangs
Some borne on stretchers dreamed of home,
Dear things, war-blotted from their hearts.

A man's brains splattered on
A stretcher-bearer's face;
His shook shoulders slipped their load,   50
But when they bent to look again
The drowning soul was sunk too deep
For human tenderness.

They left this dead with the older dead,
Stretched at the cross roads.

Burnt black by strange decay
Their sinister faces lie,
The lid over each eye;
The grass and coloured clay
More motion have than they,   60
Joined to the great sunk silences.

Here is one not long dead.
His dark hearing caught our far wheels,
And the choked soul stretched weak hands
To reach the living word the far wheels said;
The blood-dazed intelligence beating for light,
Crying through the suspense of the far torturing wheels
Swift for the end to break
Or the wheels to break,
Cried as the tide of the world broke over his sight,   70
'Will they come? Will they ever come?'
Even as the mixed hoofs of the mules,
The quivering-bellied mules,
And the rushing wheels all mixed
With his tortured upturned sight.

So we crashed round the bend,
We heard his weak scream,
We heard his very last sound,
And our wheels grazed his dead face.

Isaac Rosenberg

Youth in Arms IV: Carrion

It is plain now what you are. Your head has dropped
Into a furrow. And the lovely curve
Of your strong leg has wasted and is propped
Against a ridge of the ploughed land's watery swerve.

You are swayed on waves of the silent ground;
You clutch and claim with passionate grasp of your
    fingers
The dip of earth in which your body lingers;
If you are not found,
In a little while your limbs will fall apart;
The birds will take some, but the earth will take most
    of your heart.   10

You are fuel for a coming spring if they leave you here;
The crop that will rise from your bones is healthy
    bread.
You died – we know you – without a word of fear,
And as they loved you living I love you dead.

No girl would kiss you. But then
No girls would ever kiss the earth
In the manner they hug the lips of men:
You are not known to them in this, your second birth.

No coffin-cover now will cram
Your body in a shell of lead;   20
Earth will not fall on you from the spade with a slam,
But will fold and enclose you slowly, you living dead.

Hush, I hear the guns. Are you still asleep?
Surely I saw you a little heave to reply.
I can hardly think you will not turn over and creep
Along the furrows trenchward as if to die.

Harold Monro

A Dead Boche

To you who'd read my songs of War
And only hear of blood and fame,
I'll say (you've heard it said before)
   'War's Hell!' and if you doubt the same,
To-day I found in Mametz Wood
A certain cure for lust of blood:

Where, propped against a shattered trunk,
   In a great mess of things unclean,
Sat a dead Boche; he scowled and stunk
   With clothes and face a sodden green,   10
Big-bellied, spectacled, crop-haired,
Dribbling black blood from nose and beard.

Robert Graves

Soliloquy II

I was wrong, quite wrong;
The dead men are not always carrion.

After the advance,
As we went through the shattered trenches
Which the enemy had left,
We found, lying upon the fire-step,
A dead English soldier,
His head bloodily bandaged
And his closed left hand touching the earth,

More beautiful than one can tell,   10
More subtly coloured than a perfect Goya,
And more divine and lovely in repose
Than Angelo's hand could ever carve in stone.

Richard Aldington

Butchers and Tombs

After so much battering of fire and steel
It had seemed well to cover them with Cotswold
    stone –
And shortly praising their courage and quick skill
Leave them buried, hidden till the slow, inevitable
Change came should make them service of France
    alone.
But the time's hurry, the commonness of the tale
Made it a thing not fitting ceremonial,
And so the disregarders of blister on heel,
Pack on shoulder, barrage and work at the wires,
One wooden cross had for ensign of honour and life
    gone –   10
Save when the Gloucesters turning sudden to tell to one
Some joke, would remember and say – 'That joke is
    done,'
Since he who would understand was so cold he could
    not feel,
And clay binds hard, and sandbags get rotten and
    crumble.

Ivor Gurney

A Private

This ploughman dead in battle slept out of doors
Many a frozen night, and merrily
Answered staid drinkers, good bedmen, and all bores:
'At Mrs Greenland's Hawthorn Bush,' said he,
'I slept.' None knew which bush. Above the town,
Beyond 'The Drover,' a hundred spot the down
In Wiltshire. And where now at last he sleeps
More sound in France – that, too, he secret keeps.

Edward Thomas

The Volunteer

Here lies a clerk who half his life had spent
Toiling at ledgers in a city grey,
Thinking that so his days would drift away
With no lance broken in life's tournament:
Yet ever 'twixt the books and his bright eyes
The gleaming eagles of the legions came,
And horsemen, charging under phantom skies,
Went thundering past beneath the oriflamme.

And now those waiting dreams are satisfied;
From twilight into spacious dawn he went;   10
His lance is broken; but he lies content
With that high hour, in which he lived and died.
And falling thus he wants no recompense,
Who found his battle in the last resort;
Nor needs he any hearse to bear him hence,
Who goes to join the men of Agincourt.

Herbert Asquith

In Flanders Fields

In Flanders fields the poppies blow
Between the crosses, row on row,
   That mark our place; and in the sky
   The larks, still bravely singing, fly
Scarce heard amid the guns below.

We are the Dead. Short days ago
We lived, felt dawn, saw sunset glow,
   Loved and were loved, and now we lie,
         In Flanders fields.

Take up our quarrel with the foe: 10
To you from failing hands we throw
   The torch; be yours to hold it high.
   If ye break faith with us who die
We shall not sleep, though poppies grow
         In Flanders fields.

John McCrae

1914: *The Dead*

Blow out, you bugles, over the rich Dead!
　　There's none of these so lonely and poor of old,
　　But, dying, has made us rarer gifts than gold.
These laid the world away; poured out the red
Sweet wine of youth; gave up the years to be
　　Of work and joy, and that unhoped serene,
　　That men call age; and those who would have been,
Their sons, they gave, their immortality.

Blow, bugles, blow! They brought us, for our dearth,
　　Holiness, lacked so long, and Love, and Pain. 　　　10
Honour has come back, as a king, to earth,
　　And paid his subjects with a royal wage;
And Nobleness walks in our ways again;
　　And we have come into our heritage.

Rupert Brooke

1914: *The Dead*

These hearts were woven of human joys and cares,
    Washed marvellously with sorrow, swift to mirth.
The years had given them kindness. Dawn was theirs,
    And sunset, and the colours of the earth.
These had seen movement, and heard music; known
    Slumber and waking; loved; gone proudly friended;
Felt the quick stir of wonder; sat alone;
    Touched flowers and furs and cheeks. All this is
        ended.

There are waters blown by changing winds to laughter
And lit by the rich skies, all day. And after,   10
    Frost, with a gesture, stays the waves that dance
And wandering loveliness. He leaves a white
    Unbroken glory, a gathered radiance,
A width, a shining peace, under the night.

Rupert Brooke

'When you see millions of the mouthless dead'

When you see millions of the mouthless dead
Across your dreams in pale battalions go,
Say not soft things as other men have said,
That you'll remember. For you need not so.
Give them not praise. For, deaf, how should they know
It is not curses heaped on each gashed head?
Nor tears. Their blind eyes see not your tears flow.
Nor honour. It is easy to be dead.
Say only this, 'They are dead.' Then add thereto,
'Yet many a better one has died before.'   10
Then, scanning all the o'ercrowded mass, should you
Perceive one face that you loved heretofore,
It is a spook. None wears the face you knew.
Great death has made all his for evermore.

Charles Hamilton Sorley

Strange Meeting

It seemed that out of the battle I escaped
Down some profound dull tunnel, long since scooped
Through granites which Titanic wars had groined.
Yet also there encumbered sleepers groaned,
Too fast in thought or death to be bestirred.
Then, as I probed them, one sprang up, and stared
With piteous recognition in fixed eyes,
Lifting distressful hands as if to bless.
And by his smile, I knew that sullen hall;
With a thousand fears that vision's face was grained;   10
Yet no blood reached there from the upper ground,
And no guns thumped, or down the flues made moan.
'Strange, friend,' I said, 'Here is no cause to mourn.'
'None,' said the other, 'Save the undone years,
The hopelessness. Whatever hope is yours,
Was my life also; I went hunting wild
After the wildest beauty in the world,
Which lies not calm in eyes, or braided hair,
But mocks the steady running of the hour,
And if it grieves, grieves richlier than here.   20
For by my glee might many men have laughed,
And of my weeping something has been left,
Which must die now. I mean the truth untold,
The pity of war, the pity war distilled.
Now men will go content with what we spoiled.
Or, discontent, boil bloody, and be spilled.
They will be swift with swiftness of the tigress,
None will break ranks, though nations trek from
    progress.

Courage was mine, and I had mystery;
Wisdom was mine, and I had mastery;   30
To miss the march of this retreating world
Into vain citadels that are not walled.
Then, when much blood had clogged their chariot-
        wheels
I would go up and wash them from sweet wells,
Even with truths that lie too deep for taint.
I would have poured my spirit without stint
But not through wounds; not on the cess of war.
Foreheads of men have bled where no wounds were.
I am the enemy you killed, my friend.
I knew you in this dark; for so you frowned   40
Yesterday through me as you jabbed and killed.
I parried; but my hands were loath and cold.
Let us sleep now . . .'

Wilfred Owen

Prisoners

Comrades of risk and rigour long ago
Who have done battle under honour's name,
Hoped (living or shot down) some meed of fame,
And wooed bright Danger for a thrilling kiss, –
Laugh, oh laugh well, that we have come to this!

Laugh, oh laugh loud, all ye who long ago
Adventure found in gallant company!
Safe in Stagnation, laugh, laugh bitterly,
While on this filthiest backwater of Time's flow
Drift we and rot, till something sets us free!   10

Laugh like old men with senses atrophied,
Heeding no Present, to the Future dead,
Nodding quite foolish by the warm fireside
And seeing no flame, but only in the red
And flickering embers, pictures of the past: –
Life like a cinder fading black at last.

F. W. Harvey

His Mate

'Hi-diddle-diddle
The cat and the fiddle' . . .

I raised my head,
And saw him seated on a heap of dead,
Yelling the nursery-tune,
Grimacing at the moon . . .

'And the cow jumped over the moon.
The little dog laughed to see such sport
And the dish ran away with the spoon.'

And, as he stopt to snigger,   10
I struggled to my knees and pulled the trigger.

Wilfrid Gibson

Epitaphs: The Coward

I could not look on Death, which being known,
Men led me to him, blindfold and alone.

Rudyard Kipling

The Deserter

'I'm sorry I done it, Major.'
We bandaged the livid face;
And led him, ere the wan sun rose,
To die his death of disgrace.

The bolt-heads locked to the cartridge;
The rifles steadied to rest,
As cold stock nestled at colder cheek
And foresight lined on the breast.

'*Fire!*' called the Sergeant-Major.
The muzzles flamed as he spoke: 10
And the shameless soul of a nameless man
Went up in the cordite-smoke.

Gilbert Frankau

My Boy Jack

'Have you news of my boy Jack?'
    Not this tide.
'When d'you think that he'll come back?'
    Not with this wind blowing, and this tide.

'Has any one else had word of him?'
    Not this tide.
For what is sunk will hardly swim,
    Not with this wind blowing, and this tide.

'Oh, dear, what comfort can I find?'
    None this tide,   10
    Nor any tide,
Except he did not shame his kind –
    Not even with that wind blowing, and that tide.

Then hold your head up all the more,
    This tide,
    And every tide;
Because he was the son you bore,
    And gave to that wind blowing and that tide!

Rudyard Kipling

Easter Monday

In the last letter that I had from France
You thanked me for the silver Easter egg
Which I had hidden in the box of apples
You liked to munch beyond all other fruit.
You found the egg the Monday before Easter,
And said, 'I will praise Easter Monday now –
It was such a lovely morning.' Then you spoke
Of the coming battle and said, 'This is the eve.
'Good-bye. And may I have a letter soon'.

That Easter Monday was a day for praise,   10
It was such a lovely morning. In our garden
We sowed our earliest seeds, and in the orchard
The apple-bud was ripe. It was the eve.
There are three letters that you will not get.

Eleanor Farjeon

4 BLIGHTY

Going Back

'I want to go home'

I want to go home,
I want to go home.
I don't want to go in the trenches no more,
Where the whizz-bangs and shrapnel they whistle and
    roar.
Take me over the sea,
Where the Alleyman can't get at me.
Oh my, I don't want to die,
I want to go home.

I want to go home,
I want to go home.   10
I don't want to visit la Belle France no more,
For oh the Jack Johnsons they make such a roar.
Take me over the sea,
Where the snipers they can't get at me.
Oh my, I don't want to die, I want to go home.

Soldiers' song

If We Return
(Rondeau)

If we return, will England be
Just England still to you and me?
The place where we must earn our bread?
We, who have walked among the dead.
And watched the smile of agony,

And seen the price of Liberty,
Which we have taken carelessly
From other hands. Nay, we shall dread,
If we return,

Dread lest we hold blood-guiltily   10
The things that men have died to free.
Oh, English fields shall blossom red
For all the blood that has been shed
By men whose guardians are we,
If we return.

F. W. Harvey

Blighty

It seemed that it were well to kiss first earth
On landing, having traversed the narrow seas,
And grasp so little, tenderly, of this field of birth.
France having trodden and lain on, travelled bending
　　the knees.
And having shed blood, known heart for her and last
　　nerve freeze,
Proved body past heart, and soul past (so we thought)
　　any worth.
For what so dear a thing as the first homecoming,
The seeing smoke pillar aloft from the home dwellings;
Sign of travel ended, lifted awhile the dooming
Sentence of exile; homecoming, right of tale-tellings?　10
But mud is on our fate after so long acquaintance,
We find of England the first gate without Romance;
Blue paved wharfs with dock-policemen and civic
　　decency,
Trains and restrictions, order and politeness and
　　directions,
Motion by black and white, guided ever about-ways
And staleness with petrol-dust distinguishing days.
A grim faced black-garbed mother efficient and busy
Set upon housework, worn-minded and fantasy free –
A work-house matron, forgetting her old birth friend –
　　the sea.

Ivor Gurney

War Girls

There's the girl who clips your ticket for the train,
  And the girl who speeds the lift from floor to floor,
There's the girl who does a milk-round in the rain,
  And the girl who calls for orders at your door.
      Strong, sensible, and fit,
      They're out to show their grit,
    And tackle jobs with energy and knack.
      No longer caged and penned up,
      They're going to keep their end up
  Till the khaki soldier boys come marching back.   10

There's the motor girl who drives a heavy van,
  There's the butcher girl who brings your joint of meat,
There's the girl who cries 'All fares, please!' like a man,
  And the girl who whistles taxis up the street.
      Beneath each uniform
      Beats a heart that's soft and warm,
    Though of canny mother-wit they show no lack;
      But a solemn statement this is,
      They've no time for love and kisses
  Till the khaki soldier boys come marching back.   20

Jessie Pope

Home Service

'At least it wasn't your fault' I hear them console
When they come back, the few that will come back.
I feel those handshakes now. 'Well, on the whole
You didn't miss much. I wish I had your knack
Of stopping out. You can still call your soul
Your own, at any rate. What a priceless slack
You've had, old chap. It must have been top-hole.
How's poetry? I bet you've written a stack.'

What shall I say? That it's been damnable?
That all the time my soul was never my own? 10
That we've slaved hard at endless make-believe?
It isn't only actual war that's hell,
I'll say. It's spending youth and hope alone
Among pretences that have ceased to deceive.

Geoffrey Faber

The Survivor Comes Home

Despair and doubt in the blood:
Autumn, a smell rotten-sweet:
What stirs in the drenching wood?
What drags at my heart, my feet?
What stirs in the wood?

Nothing stirs, nothing cries.
Run weasel, cry bird for me,
Comfort my ears, soothe my eyes!
Horror on ground, over tree!
Nothing calls, nothing flies.   10

Once in a blasted wood,
A shrieking fevered waste,
We jeered at Death where he stood:
I jeered, I too had a taste
Of Death in the wood.

Am I alive and the rest
Dead, all dead? sweet friends
With the sun they have journeyed west;
For me now night never ends,
A night without rest.   20

Death, your revenge is ripe.
Spare me! but can Death spare?
Must I leap, howl to your pipe
Because I denied you there?
Your vengeance is ripe.

Death, ay, terror of Death:
If I laughed at you, scorned you now
You flash in my eyes, choke my breath . . .
'Safe home.' Safe? Twig and bough
Drip, drip, drip with Death!   30

Robert Graves

Sick Leave

When I'm asleep, dreaming and lulled and warm, –
They come, the homeless ones, the noiseless dead.
While the dim charging breakers of the storm
Bellow and drone and rumble overhead,
Out of the gloom they gather about my bed.
    They whisper to my heart; their thoughts are mine.
    'Why are you here with all your watches ended?
    From Ypres to Frise we sought you in the Line.'
In bitter safety I awake, unfriended;
And while the dawn begins with slashing rain   10
I think of the Battalion in the mud.
'When are you going out to them again?
Are they not still your brothers through our blood?'

Siegfried Sassoon

Reserve

Though you desire me I will still feign sleep
And check my eyes from opening to the day,
For as I lie, thrilled by your gold-dark flesh,
I think of how the dead, my dead, once lay.

Richard Aldington

Wife and Country

Dear, let me thank you for this:
That you made me remember, in fight,
    England – all mine at your kiss,
At the touch of your hands in the night:
    England – your giving's delight.

Gilbert Frankau

Girl to Soldier on Leave

I love you – Titan lover,
My own storm-days' Titan.
Greater than the son of Zeus,
I know whom I would choose.

Titan – my splendid rebel –
The old Prometheus
Wanes like a ghost before your power –
His pangs were joys to yours.

Pallid days arid and wan
Tied your soul fast.   10
Babel-cities' smoky tops
Pressed upon your growth

Weary gyves. What were you
But a word in the brain's ways,
Or the sleep of Circe's swine?
One gyve holds you yet.

It held you hiddenly on the Somme
Tied from my heart at home.
O must it loosen now? I wish
You were bound with the old old gyves.   20

Love! you love me – your eyes
Have looked through death at mine.
You have tempted a grave too much.
I let you – I repine.

Isaac Rosenberg

The Pavement

In bitter London's heart of stone,
    Under the lamplight's shielded glare
I saw a soldier's body thrown
    Unto the drabs that traffic there

Pacing the pavements with slow feet:
    Those old pavements whose blown dust
Throttles the hot air of the street,
    And the darkness smells of lust.

The chaste moon, with equal glance,
    Looked down on the mad world, astare   10
At those who conquered in sad France
    And those who perished in Leicester Square.

And in her light his lips were pale:
    Lips that love had moulded well:
Out of the jaws of Passchendaele
    They had sent him to this nether hell.

I had no stone of scorn to fling,
    For I know not how the wrong began –
But I had seen a hateful thing
    Masked in the dignity of man: 20

And hate and sorrow and hopeless anger
    Swept my heart, as the winds that sweep
Angrily through the leafless hanger
    When winter rises from the deep . . .

*

I would that war were what men dream:
　A crackling fire, a cleansing flame,
That it might leap the space between
　And lap up London and its shame.

Francis Brett Young

Not to Keep

They sent him back to her. The letter came
Saying . . . And she could have him. And before
She could be sure there was no hidden ill
Under the formal writing, he was in her sight,
Living. They gave him back to her alive –
How else? They are not known to send the dead –
And not disfigured visibly. His face?
His hands? She had to look, to ask,
'What is it, dear?' And she had given all
And still she had all – *they* had – they the lucky!   10
Wasn't she glad now? Everything seemed won,
And all the rest for them permissible ease.
She had to ask, 'What was it, dear?'

        'Enough,
Yet not enough. A bullet through and through,
High in the breast. Nothing but what good care
And medicine and rest, and you a week,
Can cure me of to go again.' The same
Grim giving to do over for them both.
She dared no more than ask him with her eyes   20
How was it with him for a second trial.
And with his eyes he asked her not to ask.
They had given him back to her, but not to keep.

Robert Frost

Going Back

The night turns slowly round,
Swift trains go by in a rush of light;
Slow trains steal past.
This train beats anxiously, outward bound.

But I am not here.
I am away, beyond the scope of this turning;
There, where the pivot is, the axis
Of all this gear.

I, who sit in tears,
I, whose heart is torn with parting;   10
Who cannot bear to think back to the departure platform;
My spirit hears

Voices of men,
Sound of artillery, aeroplanes, presences,
And more than all, the dead-sure silence,
The pivot again.

There, at the axis
Pain, or love, or grief
Sleep on speed; in dead certainty;
Pure relief.   20

There, at the pivot
Time sleeps again.
No has-been, no here-after, only the perfected
Silence of men.

D. H. Lawrence

The Other War

'I wore a tunic'

I wore a tunic,
A dirty khaki-tunic,
And you wore civilian clothes.
We fought and bled at Loos
While you were on the booze,
The booze that no one here knows.
Oh, you were with the wenches
While we were in the trenches
Facing the German foe.
Oh, you were a-slacking   10
While we were attacking
Down the Menin Road.

Soldiers' song

'Blighters'

The House is crammed: tier beyond tier they grin
And cackle at the Show, while prancing ranks
Of harlots shrill the chorus, drunk with din;
'We're sure the Kaiser loves the dear old Tanks!'

I'd like to see a Tank come down the stalls,
Lurching to rag-time tunes, or 'Home, Sweet Home,' –
And there'd be no more jokes in Music-halls
To mock the riddled corpses round Bapaume.

Siegfried Sassoon

Ragtime

A minx in khaki struts the limelit boards:
With false moustache, set smirk, and ogling eyes
And straddling legs and swinging hips she tries
To swagger it like a soldier, while the chords
Of rampant ragtime jangle, clash and clatter,
And over the brassy blare and drumming din
She strains to squirt her squeaky notes and thin
Spittle of sniggering lascivious patter.

Then out into the jostling Strand I turn,
And down a dark lane to the quiet river,   10
One stream of silver under the full moon,
And think of how cold searchlights flare and burn
Over dank trenches where men crouch and shiver,
Humming, to keep their hearts up, that same tune.

Wilfrid Gibson

Ragtime

The lamps glow here and there, then echo down
The vast deserted vistas of the town –
Each light the echo'd note of some refrain
Repeated in the city's fevered brain.
Yet all is still, save when there wanders past
– Finding the silence of the night too long –
Some tattered wretch, who, from the night outcast,
Sings, with an aching heart, a comic song.
The vapid parrot-words flaunt through the night –
Silly and gay, yet terrible. We know   10
Men sang these words in many a deadly fight,
And threw them – laughing – to a solemn foe;
Sang them where tattered houses stand up tall and
    stark,
And bullets whistle through the ruined street,
Where live men tread on dead men in the dark,
And skulls are sown in fields once sown with wheat.
Across the sea, where night is dark with blood
And rockets flash, and guns roar hoarse and deep,
They struggle through entanglements and mud,
They suffer wounds – and die –   20
                    But here they sleep.
From far away the outcast's vacuous song
Re-echoes like the singing of a throng;
His dragging footfalls echo down the street,
And turn into a myriad marching feet.

Osbert Sitwell

The Admonition: To Betsey

Remember, on your knees,
The men who guard your slumbers –

And guard a house in a still street
Of drifting leaves and drifting feet,
A deep blue window where below
Lies moonlight on the roofs like snow,
A clock that still the quarters tells
To the dove that roosts beneath the bell's
Grave canopy of silent brass
Round which the little night winds pass   10
Yet stir it not in the grey steeple;
And guard all small and drowsy people
Whom gentlest dusk doth disattire,
Undressing by the nursery fire
In unperturbed numbers
On this side of the seas –

Remember, on your knees,
The men who guard your slumbers.

Helen Parry Eden

Air-Raid

Night shatters in mid-heaven: the bark of guns,
The roar of planes, the crash of bombs, and all
The unshackled skiey pandemonium stuns
The senses to indifference, when a fall
Of masonry nearby startles awake,
Tingling, wide-eyed, prick-eared, with bristling hair,
Each sense within the body, crouched aware
Like some sore-hunted creature in the brake.

Yet side by side we lie in the little room
Just touching hands, with eyes and ears that strain   10
Keenly, yet dream-bewildered, through tense gloom,
Listening, in helpless stupor of insane
Cracked nightmare panic, fantastically wild,
To the quiet breathing of our sleeping child.

Wilfrid Gibson

Zeppelins

I saw the people climbing up the street
Maddened with war and strength and thought to kill;
And after followed Death, who held with skill
His torn rags royally, and stamped his feet.

The fires flamed up and burnt the serried town,
Most where the sadder, poorer houses were;
Death followed with proud feet and smiling stare,
And the mad crowds ran madly up and down.

And many died and hid in unfound places
In the black ruins of the frenzied night;   10
And Death still followed in his surplice, white
And streaked in imitation of their faces.

*

But in the morning, men began again
To mock Death following in bitter pain.

Nancy Cunard

'Education'

The rain is slipping, dripping down the street;
The day is grey as ashes on the hearth.
The children play with soldiers made of tin,
　　　While you sew
　　　Row after row.

The tears are slipping, dripping one by one;
Your son has shot and wounded his small brother.
The mimic battle's ended with a sob,
　　　While you dream
　　　Over your seam.　　　　　　　　　　　　　　　10

The blood is slipping, dripping drop by drop;
The men are dying in the trenches' mud.
The bullets search the quick among the dead.
　　　While you drift,
　　　The Gods sift.

The ink is slipping, dripping from the pens,
On papers, White and Orange, Red and Grey, –
History for the children of to-morrow, –
　　　While you prate
　　　About Fate.　　　　　　　　　　　　　　　20

War is slipping, dripping death on earth.
If the child is father of the man,
Is the toy gun father of the Krupps?
       For Christ's sake think!
       While you sew
       Row after row.

Pauline Barrington

Socks

Shining pins that dart and click
   In the fireside's sheltered peace
Check the thoughts that cluster thick –
   20 plain and then decrease.

He was brave – well, so was I –
   Keen and merry, but his lip
Quivered when he said good-bye –
   Purl the seam-stitch, purl and slip.

Never used to living rough,
   Lots of things he'd got to learn;   10
Wonder if he's warm enough –
   Knit 2, catch 2, knit 1, turn.

Hark! The paper-boys again!
   Wish that shout could be suppressed;
Keeps one always on the strain –
   Knit off 9, and slip the rest.

Wonder if he's fighting now,
   What he's done and where he's been;
He'll come out on top, somehow –
   Slip 1, knit 2, purl 14.   20

Jessie Pope

A War Film

I saw,
With a catch of the breath and the heart's uplifting,
Sorrow and pride,
    The 'week's great draw' –
The Mons Retreat;
The 'Old Contemptibles' who fought, and died,
The horror and the anguish and the glory.

As in a dream,
Still hearing machine-guns rattle and shells scream,
I came out into the street.   10

When day was done,
My little son
Wondered at bath-time why I kissed him so,
Naked upon my knee.
How could he know
The sudden terror that assaulted me? . . .
The body I had borne
Nine moons beneath my heart,
A part of me . . .
If, someday,   20
It should be taken away
To War. Tortured. Torn.
Slain.
Rotting in No Man's Land, out in the rain –
My little son . . .
Yet all those men had mothers, every one.

How should he know
Why I kissed and kissed and kissed him, crooning his
    name?
He thought that I was daft.
He thought it was a game, 30
And laughed, and laughed.

Theresa Hooley

The War Films

O living pictures of the dead,
   O songs without a sound,
O fellowship whose phantom tread
   Hallows a phantom ground –
How in a gleam have these revealed
   The faith we had not found.

We have sought God in a cloudy Heaven,
   We have passed by God on earth:
His seven sins and his sorrows seven,
   His wayworn mood and mirth,   10
Like a ragged cloak have hid from us
   The secret of his birth.

Brother of men, when now I see
   The lads go forth in line,
Thou knowest my heart is hungry in me
   As for thy bread and wine:
Thou knowest my heart is bowed in me
   To take their death for mine.

Sir Henry Newbolt

The Dancers
(During a Great Battle, 1916)

The floors are slippery with blood:
The world gyrates too. God is good
That while His wind blows out the light
For those who die hourly for us –
We can still dance, each night.

The music has grown numb with death –
But we will suck their dying breath,
The whispered name they breathed to chance,
To swell our music, make it loud
That we may dance, – may dance.   10

We are the dull blind carrion-fly
That dance and batten. Though God die
Mad from the horror of the light –
The light is mad, too, flecked with blood, –
We dance, we dance, each night.

Edith Sitwell

Epitaphs: A Son

My son was killed while laughing at some jest. I would
   I knew
What it was, and it might serve me in a time when jests
   are few.

Rudyard Kipling

'I looked up from my writing'

I looked up from my writing,
    And gave a start to see,
As if rapt in my inditing,
    The moon's full gaze on me.

Her meditative misty head
    Was spectral in its air,
And I involuntarily said,
    'What are you doing there?'

'Oh, I've been scanning pond and hole
    And waterway hereabout   10
For the body of one with a sunken soul
    Who has put his life-light out.

'Did you hear his frenzied tattle?
    It was sorrow for his son
Who is slain in brutish battle,
    Though he has injured none.

'And now I am curious to look
    Into the blinkered mind
Of one who wants to write a book
    In a world of such a kind.'   20

Her temper overwrought me,
    And I edged to shun her view,
For I felt assured she thought me
    One who should drown him too.

Thomas Hardy

Picnic
July 1917

We lay and ate sweet hurt-berries
  In the bracken of Hurt Wood.
Like a quire of singers singing low
  The dark pines stood.

Behind us climbed the Surrey hills,
  Wild, wild in greenery;
At our feet the downs of Sussex broke
  To an unseen sea.

And life was bound in a still ring,
  Drowsy, and quiet, and sweet . . .   10
When heavily up the south-east wind
  The great guns beat.

We did not wince, we did not weep,
  We did not curse or pray;
We drowsily heard, and someone said,
  'They sound clear to-day'.

We did not shake with pity and pain,
  Or sicken and blanch white.
We said, 'If the wind's from over there
  There'll be rain to-night'.   20

*

Once pity we knew, and rage we knew,
  And pain we knew, too well,

197

As we stared and peered dizzily
    Through the gates of hell.

But now hell's gates are an old tale;
    Remote the anguish seems;
The guns are muffled and far away,
    Dreams within dreams.

And far and far are Flanders mud,
    And the pain of Picardy;   30
And the blood that runs there runs beyond
    The wide waste sea.

We are shut about by guarding walls:
    (We have built them lest we run
Mad from dreaming of naked fear
    And of black things done.)

We are ringed all round by guarding walls,
    So high, they shut the view.
Not all the guns that shatter the world
    Can quite break through.   40

                            *

Oh, guns of France, oh, guns of France
    Be still, you crash in vain . . .
Heavily up the south wind throb
    Dull dreams of pain, . . .

Be still, be still, south wind, lest your
    Blowing should bring the rain . . .

We'll lie very quiet on Hurt Hill,
    And sleep once again.

Oh, we'll lie quite still, nor listen nor look,
    While the earth's bounds reel and shake,   50
Lest, battered too long, our walls and we
    Should break . . . should break . . .

Rose Macaulay

As the Team's Head-Brass

As the team's head-brass flashed out on the turn
The lovers disappeared into the wood.
I sat among the boughs of the fallen elm
That strewed an angle of the fallow, and
Watched the plough narrowing a yellow square
Of charlock. Every time the horses turned
Instead of treading me down, the ploughman leaned
Upon the handles to say or ask a word,
About the weather, next about the war.
Scraping the share he faced towards the wood,   10
And screwed along the furrow till the brass flashed
Once more.
                    The blizzard felled the elm whose crest
I sat in, by a woodpecker's round hole,
The ploughman said. 'When will they take it away?'
'When the war's over.' So the talk began –
One minute and an interval of ten,
A minute more and the same interval.
'Have you been out?' 'No.' 'And don't want to,
      perhaps?'
'If I could only come back again, I should.   20
I could spare an arm. I shouldn't want to lose
A leg. If I should lose my head, why, so,
I should want nothing more . . . Have many gone
From here?' 'Yes.' 'Many lost?' 'Yes: good few.
Only two teams work on the farm this year.
One of my mates is dead. The second day
In France they killed him. It was back in March,
The very night of the blizzard, too. Now if

He had stayed here we should have moved the tree.'
'And I should not have sat here. Everything   30
Would have been different. For it would have been
Another world.' 'Ay, and a better, though
If we could see all all might seem good.' Then
The lovers came out of the wood again:
The horses started and for the last time
I watched the clods crumble and topple over
After the ploughshare and the stumbling team.

Edward Thomas

The Farmer, 1917

I see a farmer walking by himself
In the ploughed field, returning like the day
To his dark nest. The plovers circle round
In the gray sky; the blackbird calls; the thrush
Still sings – but all the rest have gone to sleep.
I see the farmer coming up the field,
Where the new corn is sown, but not yet sprung;
He seems to be the only man alive
And thinking through the twilight of this world.
I know that there is war behind those hills,   10
And I surmise, but cannot see the dead,
And cannot see the living in their midst –
So awfully and madly knit with death.
I cannot feel, but I know there is war,
And has been now for three eternal years,
Behind the subtle cinctures of those hills.
I see the farmer coming up the field,
And as I look, imagination lifts
The sullen veil of alternating cloud,
And I am stunned by what I see behind   20
His solemn and uncompromising form:
Wide hosts of men who once could walk like him
In freedom, quite alone with night and day,
Uncounted shapes of living flesh and bone,
Worn dull, quenched dry, gone blind and sick, with
    war;
And they are him and he is one with them;
They see him as he travels up the field.
O God, how lonely freedom seems to-day!

O single farmer walking through the world,
They bless the seed in you that earth shall reap,   30
When they, their countless lives, and all their thoughts,
Lie scattered by the storm: when peace shall come
With stillness, and long shivers, after death.

Fredegond Shove

May, 1915

Let us remember Spring will come again
      To the scorched, blackened woods, where
        the wounded trees
Wait with their old wise patience for the heavenly
      rain,
Sure of the sky: sure of the sea to send its healing
      breeze,
      Sure of the sun. And even as to these
        Surely the Spring, when God shall please,
      Will come again like a divine surprise
To those who sit to-day with their great Dead, hands in
      their hands, eyes in their eyes,
At one with Love, at one with Grief: blind to the
      scattered things and changing skies.

Charlotte Mew

Lucky Blighters

'They'

The Bishop tells us: 'When the boys come back
They will not be the same; for they'll have fought
In a just cause: they lead the last attack
On Anti-Christ; their comrades' blood has bought
New right to breed an honourable race.
They have challenged Death and dared him face to
    face.'

'We're none of us the same!' the boys reply.
'For George lost both his legs; and Bill's stone blind;
Poor Jim's shot through the lungs and like to die;
And Bert's gone siphilitic: you'll not find   10
A chap who's served that hasn't found *some* change.'
And the Bishop said: 'The ways of God are strange!'

Siegfried Sassoon

Portrait of a Coward

True he'd have fought to death if the Germans came –
But an hours battering after a days battering
Brought his soul down to quivering, with small shame.
And he was fit to run, if his chance had come.
But Gloucesters of more sterner frame and spirit
Kept him in place without reproach, (sweet blood
    inherit
From hills and nature) said no word and kept him
    there.
True, he'd have fought to death, but Laventie's needing
Was a nerve to hide the pain of the soul bleeding –
Say nothing, and nothing ever of God to beg.   10
He hurt more, did fatigues, and was friend to share
What food was not his need; of enemies not heeding.
Everybody was glad – (but determined to hide the bad)
When he took courage at wiremending and shot his leg,
And got to Blighty, no man saying word of denying.

Ivor Gurney

In A Soldiers' Hospital I: Pluck

Crippled for life at seventeen,
　　His great eyes seem to question why:
With both legs smashed it might have been
　　Better in that grim trench to die
　　Than drag maimed years out helplessly.

A child – so wasted and so white,
　　He told a lie to get his way,
To march, a man with men, and fight
　　While other boys are still at play.
　　A gallant lie your heart will say.　　　　　10

So broke with pain, he shrinks in dread
　　To see the 'dresser' drawing near;
And winds the clothes about his head
　　That none may see his heart-sick fear.
　　His shaking, strangled sobs you hear.

But when the dreaded moment's there
　　He'll face us all, a soldier yet,
Watch his bared wounds with unmoved air,
　　(Though tell-tale lashes still are wet,)
　　And smoke his woodbine cigarette.　　　　　20

Eva Dobell

In A Soldiers' Hospital II: Gramophone Tunes

Through the long ward the gramophone
   Grinds out its nasal melodies:
'Where did you get that girl?' it shrills.
   The patients listen at their ease,
Through clouds of strong tobacco-smoke:
   The gramophone can always please.

The Welsh boy has it by his bed,
   (He's lame – one leg was blown away.)
He'll lie propped up with pillows there,
   And wind the handle half the day.   10
His neighbour, with the shattered arm,
   Picks out the records he must play.

Jock with his crutches beats the time;
   The gunner, with his head close-bound,
Listens with puzzled, patient smile:
   (Shell-shock – he cannot hear a sound.)
The others join in from their beds,
   And send the chorus rolling round.

Somehow for me these common tunes
   Can never sound the same again: 20
They've magic now to thrill my heart
   And bring before me, clear and plain,
Man that is master of his flesh,
   And has the laugh of death and pain.

Eva Dobell

Hospital Sanctuary

When you have lost your all in a world's upheaval,
Suffered and prayed, and found your prayers were vain,
When love is dead, and hope has no renewal –
These need you still; come back to them again.

When the sad days bring you the loss of all ambition,
And pride is gone that gave you strength to bear,
When dreams are shattered, and broken is all decision –
Turn you to these, dependent on your care.

They too have fathomed the depths of human anguish,
Seen all that counted flung like chaff away;   10
The dim abodes of pain wherein they languish
Offer that peace for which at last you pray.

Vera Brittain

Convalescence

From out the dragging vastness of the sea,
    Wave-fettered, bound in sinuous, seaweed strands,
    He toils toward the rounding beach, and stands
One moment, white and dripping, silently,
Cut like a cameo in lazuli,
    Then falls, betrayed by shifting shells, and lands
    Prone in the jeering water, and his hands
Clutch for support where no support can be.
    So up, and down, and forward, inch by inch,
He gains upon the shore, where poppies glow   10
And sandflies dance their little lives away.
    The sucking waves retard, and tighter clinch
The weeds about him, but the land-winds blow,
And in the sky there blooms the sun of May.

Amy Lowell

Smile, Smile, Smile

Head to limp head, the sunk-eyed wounded scanned
Yesterday's Mail; the casualties (typed small)
And (large) Vast Booty from our Latest Haul.
Also, they read of Cheap Homes, not yet planned;
For, said the paper, 'When this war is done
The men's first instinct will be making homes.
Meanwhile their foremost need is aerodromes,
It being certain war has just begun.
Peace would do wrong to our undying dead, –
The sons we offered might regret they died   10
If we got nothing lasting in their stead.
We must be solidly indemnified.
Though all be worthy Victory which all bought,
We rulers sitting in this ancient spot
Would wrong our very selves if we forgot
The greatest glory will be theirs who fought,
Who kept this nation in integrity.'
Nation? – The half-limbed readers did not chafe
But smiled at one another curiously
Like secret men who know their secret safe.   20
This is the thing they know and never speak,
That England one by one had fled to France
(Not many elsewhere now save under France).
Pictures of these broad smiles appear each week,
And people in whose voice real feeling rings
Say: How they smile! They're happy now, poor things.

Wilfred Owen

The Beau Ideal

Since Rose a classic taste possessed,
    It naturally follows
Her girlish fancy was obsessed
    With Belvidere Apollos.
And when she dreamed about a mate,
    If any hoped to suit, he
Must in his person illustrate
    A type of manly beauty.

He must be physically fit,
    A graceful, stalwart figure,   10
Of iron and elastic knit
    And full of verve and vigour.
Enough! I've made the bias plain
    That warped her heart and thrilled it.
It was a maggot of her brain,
    And Germany has killed it.

To-day, the sound in wind and limb
    Don't flutter Rose one tittle.
Her maiden ardour cleaves to him
    Who's proved that he is brittle,   20
Whose healing cicatrices show
    The colours of a prism,
Whose back is bent into a bow
    By Flanders rheumatism.

The lad who troth with Rose would plight,
    Nor apprehend rejection,

Must be in shabby khaki dight
    To compass her affection.
Who buys her an engagement ring
    And finds her kind and kissing,   30
Must have one member in a sling
    Or, preferably, missing.

Jessie Pope

The Veteran

We came upon him sitting in the sun,
    Blinded by war, and left. And past the fence
There came young soldiers from the *Hand and Flower*,
    Asking advice of his experience.

And he said this, and that, and told them tales,
    And all the nightmares of each empty head
Blew into air; then, hearing us beside,
    'Poor chaps, how'd they know what it's like?' he said.

We stood there, and watched him as he sat,
    Turning his sockets where they went away,   10
Until it came to one of us to ask
    'And you're – how old?'
        'Nineteen, the third of May.'

Margaret Postgate Cole

Repression of War Experience

Now light the candles; one; two; there's a moth;
What silly beggars they are to blunder in
And scorch their wings with glory, liquid flame –
No, no, not that, – it's bad to think of war,
When thoughts you've gagged all day come back to
    scare you;
And it's been proved that soldiers don't go mad
Unless they lose control of ugly thoughts
That drive them out to jabber among the trees.

Now light your pipe; look, what a steady hand.
Draw a deep breath; stop thinking; count fifteen,   10
And you're as right as rain . . .
                    Why won't it rain? . . .
I wish there'd be a thunder-storm to-night,
With bucketsful of water to sluice the dark,
And make the roses hang their dripping heads.
Books; what a jolly company they are,
Standing so quiet and patient on their shelves,
Dressed in dim brown, and black, and white, and
    green,
And every kind of colour. Which will you read?
Come on; O *do* read something; they're so wise.   20
I tell you all the wisdom of the world
Is waiting for you on those shelves; and yet
You sit and gnaw your nails, and let your pipe out,
And listen to the silence: on the ceiling
There's one big, dizzy moth that bumps and flutters;
And in the breathless air outside the house

The garden waits for something that delays.
There must be crowds of ghosts among the trees, –
Not people killed in battle, – they're in France, –
But horrible shapes in shrouds – old men who died   30
Slow, natural deaths, – old men with ugly souls,
Who wore their bodies out with nasty sins.

                              *

You're quiet and peaceful, summering safe at home;
You'd never think there was a bloody war on! . . .
O yes, you would . . . why, you can hear the guns.
Hark! Thud, thud, thud, – quite soft . . . they never
    cease –
Those whispering guns – O Christ, I want to go out
And screech at them to stop – I'm going crazy;
I'm going stark, staring mad because of the guns.

                                        Siegfried Sassoon

A Child's Nightmare

Through long nursery nights he stood
By my bed unwearying,
Loomed gigantic, formless, queer,
Purring in my haunted ear
That same hideous nightmare thing,
Talking, as he lapped my blood,
In a voice cruel and flat,
Saying for ever, 'Cat! . . . Cat! . . . Cat! . . .'

That one word was all he said,
That one word through all my sleep,
In monotonous mock despair.
Nonsense may be light as air,
But there's Nonsense that can keep
Horror bristling round the head,
When a voice cruel and flat
Says for ever, 'Cat! . . . Cat! . . . Cat! . . .'

He had faded, he was gone
Years ago with Nursery Land,
When he leapt on me again
From the clank of a night train,
Overpowered me foot and head,
Lapped my blood, while on and on
The old voice cruel and flat
Purred for ever, 'Cat! . . . Cat! . . . Cat! . . .'

Morphia drowsed, again I lay
In a crater by High Wood:
He was there with straddling legs,
Staring eyes as big as eggs,
Purring as he lapped my blood,
His black bulk darkening the day,   30
With a voice cruel and flat,
'Cat! . . . Cat! . . . Cat! . . .' he said, 'Cat! . . . Cat! . . .'

When I'm shot through heart and head,
And there's no choice but to die,
The last word I'll hear, no doubt,
Won't be 'Charge!' or 'Bomb them out!'
Nor the stretcher-bearer's cry,
'Let that body be, he's dead!'
But a voice cruel and flat
Saying for ever, 'Cat! . . . Cat! . . . Cat!'   40

Robert Graves

Mental Cases

Who are these? Why sit they here in twilight?
Wherefore rock they, purgatorial shadows,
Drooping tongues from jaws that slob their relish,
Baring teeth that leer like skulls' tongues wicked?
Stroke on stroke of pain, – but what slow panic,
Gouged these chasms round their fretted sockets?
Ever from their hair and through their hand palms
Misery swelters. Surely we have perished
Sleeping, and walk hell; but who these hellish?

– These are men whose minds the Dead have   10
   ravished.
Memory fingers in their hair of murders,
Multitudinous murders they once witnessed.
Wading sloughs of flesh these helpless wander,
Treading blood from lungs that had loved laughter.
Always they must see these things and hear them,
Batter of guns and shatter of flying muscles,
Carnage incomparable and human squander
Rucked too thick for these men's extrication.

Therefore still their eyeballs shrink tormented
Back into their brains, because on their sense   20
Sunlight seems a bloodsmear; night comes blood-black;
Dawn breaks open like a wound that bleeds afresh
– Thus their heads wear this hilarious, hideous,

Awful falseness of set-smiling corpses.
– Thus their hands are plucking at each other;
Picking at the rope-knouts of their scourging;
Snatching after us who smote them, brother,
Pawing us who dealt them war and madness.

Wilfred Owen

The Death-Bed

He drowsed and was aware of silence heaped
Round him, unshaken as the steadfast walls;
Aqueous like floating rays of amber light,
Soaring and quivering in the wings of sleep, –
Silence and safety; and his mortal shore
Lipped by the inward, moonless waves of death.

Someone was holding water to his mouth.
He swallowed, unresisting; moaned and dropped
Through crimson gloom to darkness; and forgot
The opiate throb and ache that was his wound.   10
Water – calm, sliding green above the weir;
Water – a sky-lit alley for his boat,
Bird-voiced, and bordered with reflected flowers
And shaken hues of summer: drifting down,
He dipped contented oars, and sighed, and slept.

Night, with a gust of wind, was in the ward,
Blowing the curtain to a glimmering curve.
Night. He was blind; he could not see the stars
Glinting among the wraiths of wandering cloud;
Queer blots of colour, purple, scarlet, green,   20
Flickered and faded in his drowning eyes.

Rain; he could hear it rustling through the dark;
Fragrance and passionless music woven as one;
Warm rain on drooping roses; pattering showers

That soak the woods; not the harsh rain that sweeps
Behind the thunder, but a trickling peace
Gently and slowly washing life away.

*

He stirred, shifting his body; then the pain
Leaped like a prowling beast, and gripped and tore
His groping dreams with grinding claws and fangs.   30
But someone was beside him; soon he lay
Shuddering because that evil thing had passed.
And death, who'd stepped toward him, paused and
    stared.

Light many lamps and gather round his bed.
Lend him your eyes, warm blood, and will to live.
Speak to him; rouse him; you may save him yet.
He's young; he hated war; how should he die
When cruel old campaigners win safe through?

But Death replied: 'I choose him.' So he went,
And there was silence in the summer night;   40
Silence and safety; and the veils of sleep.
Then, far away, the thudding of the guns.

Siegfried Sassoon

5 PEACE

Everyone Sang

'When this bloody war is over'

When this bloody war is over,
No more soldiering for me.
When I get my civvy clothes on,
Oh, how happy I shall be!
No more church parades on Sunday,
No more begging for a pass.
You can tell the Sergeant-Major
To stick his passes up his arse.

When this bloody war is over,
No more soldiering for me.
When I get my civvy clothes on,
Oh, how happy I shall be!
No more NCOs to curse me,
No more rotten army stew.
You can tell the old Cook-Sergeant,
To stick his stew right up his flue.

When this bloody war is over,
No more soldiering for me.
When I get my civvy clothes on,

Oh, how happy I shall be!
No more sergeants bawling
'Pick it up' and 'Put it down.'
If I meet the ugly bastard
I'll kick his arse all over town.

Soldiers' song

Preparations for Victory

My soul, dread not the pestilence that hags
The valley; flinch not you, my body young,
At these great shouting smokes and snarling jags
Of fiery iron; the dice may not be flung
As yet that claims you. Manly move among
These ruins, and what you must do, do well;
Look, here are gardens, there mossed boughs are
    hung
With apples whose bright cheeks none might excel,
And there's a house as yet unshattered by a shell.

'I'll do my best,' the soul makes sad reply,   10
'And I will mark the yet unmurdered tree,
The relics of dear homes that court the eye,
And yet I see them not as I would see.
Hovering between, a ghostly enemy.
Sickens the light, and poisoned, withered, wan,
The least defiled turns desperate to me.'
The body, poor unpitied Caliban,
Parches and sweats and grunts to win the name of Man.

Hours, days, eternities like swelling waves
Pass on, and still we drudge in this dark maze,   20
The bombs and coils and cans by strings of slaves
Are borne to serve the coming day of days;
Gray sleep in slimy cellars scarce allays

With its brief blank the burden. Look, we lose;
  The sky is gone, the lightless, drenching haze
  Of rainstorm chills the bone; earth, air are foes,
The black fiend leaps brick-red as life's last picture
    goes.

Edmund Blunden

'Après la guerre finie'

Après la guerre finie,
Soldat anglais parti;
Mam'selle Fransay boko pleuray
Après la guerre finie.

Après la guerre finie,
Soldat anglais parti;
Mademoiselle in the family way,
Après la guerre finie.

Après la guerre finie,
Soldat anglais parti;
Mademoiselle can go to hell
Après la guerre finie.

Soldiers' song

Everyone Sang

Everyone suddenly burst out singing;
And I was filled with such delight
As prisoned birds must find in freedom,
Winging wildly across the white
Orchards and dark-green fields; on – on – and out of
    sight.

Everyone's voice was suddenly lifted;
And beauty came like the setting sun:
My heart was shaken with tears; and horror
Drifted away . . . O, but Everyone
Was a bird; and the song was wordless; the singing
    will never be done.   10

Siegfried Sassoon

Peace Celebration

Now we can say of those who died unsung,
Unwept for, torn, 'Thank God they were not blind
Or mad! They've perished strong and young,
Missing the misery we elders find
In missing them.' With such a platitude
We try to cheer ourselves. And for each life
Laid down for us, with duty well-imbued,
With song-on-lip, in splendid soldier strife –
For sailors, too, who willingly were sunk –
We'll shout 'Hooray!' –   10
               And get a little drunk.

Osbert Sitwell

Paris, November 11, 1918

Down the boulevards the crowds went by,
The shouting and the singing died away,
And in the quiet we rose to drink the toasts,
Our hearts uplifted to the hour, the Day:
The King – the Army – Navy – the Allies –
England – and Victory. –
And then you turned to me and with low voice
(The tables were abuzz with revelry),
'I have a toast for you and me', you said,
And whispered 'Absent', and we drank   10
Our unforgotten Dead.
  But I saw Love go lonely down the years,
  And when I drank, the wine was salt with tears.

May Wedderburn Cannan

It Is Near Toussaints

It is near Toussaints, the living and dead will say:
'Have they ended it? What has happened to Gurney?'
And along the leaf-strewed roads of France many
    brown shades
Will go, recalling singing, and a comrade for whom
    also they
Had hoped well. His honour them had happier made.
Curse all that hates good. When I spoke of my
    breaking
(Not understood) in London, they imagined of the
    taking
Vengeance, and seeing things were different in future.
(A musician was a cheap, honourable and nice
    creature.)
Kept sympathetic silence; heard their packs creaking   10
And burst into song – Hilaire Belloc was all our
    Master.
On the night of the dead, they will remember me,
Pray Michael, Nicholas, Maries lost in Novembery
River-mist in the old City of our dear love, and batter
At doors about the farms crying 'Our war poet is lost
Madame – no bon!' – and cry his two names,
    warningly, sombrely.

Ivor Gurney

Two Fusiliers

And have we done with War at last?
Well, we've been lucky devils both,
And there's no need of pledge or oath
To bind our lovely friendship fast,
By firmer stuff
Close bound enough.

By wire and wood and stake we're bound,
By Fricourt and by Festubert,
By whipping rain, by the sun's glare,
By all the misery and loud sound,   10
By a Spring day,
By Picard clay.

Show me the two so closely bound
As we, by the wet bond of blood,
By friendship, blossoming from mud,
By Death: we faced him, and we found
Beauty in Death,
In dead men breath.

Robert Graves

Report on Experience

I have been young, and now am not too old;
And I have seen the righteous forsaken,
His health, his honour and his quality taken.
    This is not what we were formerly told.

I have seen a green country, useful to the race,
Knocked silly with guns and mines, its villages vanished,
Even the last rat and last kestrel banished –
    God bless us all, this was peculiar grace.

I knew Seraphina; Nature gave her hue,
Glance, sympathy, note, like one from Eden.   10
I saw her smile warp, heard her lyric deaden;
    She turned to harlotry; – this I took to be new.

Say what you will, our God sees how they run.
These disillusions are His curious proving
That He loves humanity and will go on loving;
    Over there are faith, life, virtue in the sun.

Edmund Blunden

Dead and Buried

I have borne my cross through Flanders,
   Through the broken heart of France,
I have borne it through the deserts of the East;
   I have wandered, faint and longing,
   Through the human hosts that, thronging,
Swarmed to glut their grinning idols with a feast.

   I was crucified in Cambrai,
   And again outside Bapaume;
I was scourged for miles along the Albert Road,
   I was driven, pierced and bleeding,   10
   With a million maggots feeding
On the body that I carried as my load.

   I have craved a cup of water,
   Just a drop to quench my thirst,
As the routed armies ran to keep the pace;
   But no soldier made reply
   As the maddened hosts swept by,
And a sweating straggler kicked me in the face.

   There's no ecstasy of torture
   That the devils e'er devised,   20
That my soul has not endured unto the last;
   As I bore my cross of sorrow,
   For the glory of to-morrow,
Through the wilderness of battles that is past.

Yet my heart was still unbroken,
And my hope was still unquenched,
Till I bore my cross to Paris through the crowd.
Soldiers pierced me on the Aisne,
But 'twas by the river Seine
That the statesmen brake my legs and made
my shroud.   30

There they wrapped my mangled body
In fine linen of fair words,
With the perfume of a sweetly scented lie,
And they laid it in the tomb
Of the golden-mirrored room,
'Mid the many-fountained Gardens of Versailles.

With a thousand scraps of paper
They made fast the open door,
And the wise men of the Council saw it sealed.
With the seal of subtle lying,   40
They made certain of my dying,
Lest the torment of the peoples should be healed.

Then they set a guard of soldiers
Night and day beside the Tomb,
Where the body of the Prince of Peace is laid,
And the captains of the nations
Keep the sentries to their stations,
Lest the statesman's trust from Satan be betrayed.

For it isn't steel and iron
That men use to kill their God,   50
But the poison of a smooth and slimy tongue.
Steel and iron tear the body,
But it's oily sham and shoddy
That have trampled down God's *Spirit* in the dung.

G. A. Studdert Kennedy

The Dead and the Living

For the Fallen

With proud thanksgiving, a mother for her children,
England mourns for her dead across the sea.
Flesh of her flesh they were, spirit of her spirit,
Fallen in the cause of the free.

Solemn the drums thrill; Death august and royal
Sings sorrow up into immortal spheres,
There is music in the midst of desolation
And a glory that shines upon our tears.

They went with songs to the battle, they were young,
Straight of limb, true of eye, steady and aglow.   10
They were staunch to the end against odds uncounted;
They fell with their faces to the foe.

They shall grow not old, as we that are left grow old:
Age shall not weary them, nor the years condemn.
At the going down of the sun and in the morning
We will remember them.

They mingle not with their laughing comrades again;
They sit no more at familiar tables of home;
They have no lot in our labour of the day-time;
They sleep beyond England's foam.   20

But where our desires are and our hopes profound,
Felt as a well-spring that is hidden from sight,

To the innermost heart of their own land they are known
As the stars are known to the Night;

As the stars that shall be bright when we are dust
Moving in marches upon the heavenly plain,
As the stars that are starry in the time of our darkness,
To the end, to the end, they remain.

Laurence Binyon

The Cenotaph

Not yet will those measureless fields be green again
Where only yesterday the wild, sweet, blood of
    wonderful youth was shed;
There is a grave whose earth must hold too long, too
    deep a stain,
Though for ever over it we may speak as proudly as we
    may tread.
But here, where the watchers by lonely hearths from the
    thrust of an inward sword have more slowly bled,
We shall build the Cenotaph: Victory, winged, with
    Peace, winged too, at the column's head.
And over the stairway, at the foot – oh! here, leave
    desolate, passionate hands to spread
Violets, roses, and laurel, with the small, sweet,
    twinkling country things
Speaking so wistfully of other Springs,
From the little gardens of little places where son or
    sweetheart was born and bred.   10
In splendid sleep, with a thousand brothers
              To lovers – to mothers
              Here, too, lies he:
Under the purple, the green, the red,
It is all young life: it must break some women's hearts
    to see
Such a brave, gay coverlet to such a bed!
Only, when all is done and said,
God is not mocked and neither are the dead.

For this will stand in our Market-place –
                    Who'll sell, who'll buy   20
                (Will you or I
Lie to each with the better grace)?
While looking in every busy whore's and huckster's face
As they drive their bargains, is the Face
Of God: and some young, piteous, murdered face.

Charlotte Mew

The Silence

In the bleak twilight, when the roads are hoar
  And mists of early morning haunt the down,
His Mother shuts her empty cottage door
  Behind her, in the lane beyond the town:
Her slow steps on the highway frosty white
  Ring clear across the moor, and echo through
The drowsy town, to where the station's light
  Signals the 7.10 to Waterloo.

Some wintry flowers in her garden grown,
  And some frail dreams, she bears with her to-day –   10
Dreams of the lad who once had been her own,
  For whose dear sake she goes a weary way
To find in London, after journeying long,
  The Altar of Remembrance, set apart
For such as she, and join the pilgrim throng
  There, at that Mecca of the Broken Heart.

Princes and Lords in grave procession come
  With wondrous wreaths of glory for the dead;
Then the two minutes smite the City dumb,
  And memory dims her eyes with tears unshed;   20
The silence breaks, and music strange and sad
  Wails, while the Great Ones bow in homage low;
And still she knows her little homely lad
  Troubles no heart but hers in all the Show.

And when beside the blind stone's crowded base,
  'Mid the rich wreaths, she lays her wintry flowers,

She feels that, sleeping in some far-off place
    Indifferent to these interludes of ours,
No solace from this marshalled woe he drains,
    And that the stark Shrine stands more empty here   30
Than her own cottage, where the silence reigns,
    Not for brief minutes, but through all the year.

St John Adcock

Armistice Day, 1921

The hush begins. Nothing is heard
Save the arrested taxis throbbing,
And here and there an ignorant bird
And here a sentimental woman sobbing.

The statesman bares and bows his head
Before the solemn monument:
His lips, paying duty to the dead
In silence, are more than ever eloquent.

But ere the sacred silence breaks
And taxis hurry on again,   10
A faint and distant voice awakes,
Speaking the mind of a million absent men:

'Mourn not for us. Our better luck
At least has given us peace and rest.
We struggled when our moment struck
But now we understand that death knew best.

Would we be as our brothers are
Whose barrel-organs charm the town?
Ours was a better dodge by far –
We got *our* pensions in a lump sum down.   20

We, out of all, have had our pay,
There is no poverty where we lie:
The graveyard has no quarter-day,
The space is narrow but the rent not high.

No empty stomach here is found:
Unless some cheated worm complain
You hear no grumbling underground:
Oh never, never wish us back again!

Mourn not for us, but rather we
Will meet upon this solemn day   30
And in our greater liberty
Keep silent for you, a little while, and pray.'

Edward Shanks

'Out of the Mouths of Babes –'

Two children in my garden playing found
   A robin cruelly dead, in Summer hours.
I watched them get a trowel, and heap the mound,
   And bury him, and scatter over flowers.

And when their little friend was laid away,
   In lack of burial service over the dead
Before those two grave children turned to play: –
   'I hope he'll have a happy *dead* life!' one said.

What more was there to say for bird or beast?
   What more for any man is there to say?   10
What can we wish *them* better, as with priest
   And choir we ring the cross on Armistice Day?

F. W. Harvey

Memorial Tablet
(Great War)

Squire nagged and bullied till I went to fight,
(Under Lord Derby's Scheme). I died in hell –
(They called it Passchendaele). My wound was slight,
And I was hobbling back; and then a shell
Burst slick upon the duck-boards: so I fell
Into the bottomless mud, and lost the light.

At sermon-time, while Squire is in his pew,
He gives my gilded name a thoughtful stare;
For, though low down upon the list, I'm there;
'In proud and glorious memory' . . . that's my due.   10
Two bleeding years I fought in France, for Squire:
I suffered anguish that he's never guessed.
Once I came home on leave: and then went west . . .
What greater glory could a man desire?

Siegfried Sassoon

Elegy in a Country Churchyard

The men that worked for England
They have their graves at home:
And bees and birds of England
About the cross can roam.

But they that fought for England,
Following a falling star,
Alas, alas for England
They have their graves afar.

And they that rule in England,
In stately conclave met,   10
Alas, alas for England
They have no graves as yet.

G. K. Chesterton

Epitaphs: Common Form

If any question why we died,
Tell them, because our fathers lied.

Rudyard Kipling

Epitaph on an Army of Mercenaries

These, in the day when heaven was falling,
　The hour when earth's foundations fled,
Followed their mercenary calling
　And took their wages and are dead.

Their shoulders held the sky suspended;
　They stood, and earth's foundations stay;
What God abandoned, these defended,
　And saved the sum of things for pay.

A. E. Housman

On Passing the New Menin Gate

Who will remember, passing through this Gate,
The unheroic Dead who fed the guns?
Who shall absolve the foulness of their fate, –
Those doomed, conscripted, unvictorious ones?
    Crudely renewed, the Salient holds its own.
    Paid are its dim defenders by this pomp;
    Paid, with a pile of peace-complacent stone,
    The armies who endured that sullen swamp.

Here was the world's worst wound. And here with
      pride
'Their name liveth for ever,' the Gateway claims.   10
Was ever an immolation so belied
As these intolerably nameless names?
Well might the Dead who struggled in the slime
Rise and deride this sepulchre of crime.

Siegfried Sassoon

Hugh Selwyn Mauberley: V

There died a myriad,
And of the best, among them,
For an old bitch gone in the teeth,
For a botched civilisation,

Charm, smiling at the good mouth,
Quick eyes gone under earth's lid,

For two gross of broken statues,
For a few thousand battered books.

Ezra Pound

War and Peace

In sodden trenches I have heard men speak,
Though numb and wretched, wise and witty things;
And loved them for the stubbornness that clings
Longest to laughter when Death's pulleys creak;

And seeing cool nurses move on tireless feet
To do abominable things with grace,
Deemed them sweet sisters in that haunted place
Where, with child's voices, strong men howl or bleat.

Yet now those men lay stubborn courage by,
Riding dull-eyed and silent in the train   10
To old men's stools; or sell gay-coloured socks
And listen fearfully for Death; so I
Love the low-laughing girls, who now again
Go daintily, in thin and flowery frocks.

Edgell Rickword

A Generation (1917)

There was a time that's gone
And will not come again,
We knew it was a pleasant time,
How good we never dreamed.

When, for a whimsy's sake,
We'd even play with pain,
For everything awaited us
And life immortal seemed.

It seemed unending then
To forward-looking eyes,
No thought of what postponement meant
Hung dark across our mirth;

We had years and strength enough
For any enterprise,
Our numerous companionship
Were heirs to all the earth.

But now all memory
Is one ironic truth,
We look like strangers at the boys
We were so long ago;

For half of us are dead,
And half have lost their youth,
And our hearts are scarred by many griefs,
That only age should know.

J. C. Squire

Disabled

He sat in a wheeled chair, waiting for dark,
And shivered in his ghastly suit of grey,
Legless, sewn short at elbow. Through the park
Voices of boys rang saddening like a hymn,
Voices of play and pleasure after day,
Till gathering sleep had mothered them from him.

About this time Town used to swing so gay
When glow-lamps budded in the light-blue trees
And girls glanced lovelier as the air grew dim,
– In the old times, before he threw away his knees.   10
Now he will never feel again how slim
Girls' waists are, or how warm their subtle hands,
All of them touch him like some queer disease.

There was an artist silly for his face,
For it was younger than his youth, last year.
Now he is old; his back will never brace;
He's lost his colour very far from here,
Poured it down shell-holes till the veins ran dry,
And half his lifetime lapsed in the hot race,
And leap of purple spurted from his thigh.   20
One time he liked a bloodsmear down his leg,
After the matches carried shoulder-high.
It was after football, when he'd drunk a peg,
He thought he'd better join. He wonders why . . .
Someone had said he'd look a god in kilts.

That's why; and maybe, too, to please his Meg,
Aye, that was it, to please the giddy jilts,
He asked to join. He didn't have to beg;
Smiling they wrote his lie; aged nineteen years.
Germans he scarcely thought of; and no fears   30
Of Fear came yet. He thought of jewelled hilts
For daggers in plaid socks; of smart salutes;
And care of arms; and leave; and pay arrears;
Esprit de corps; and hints for young recruits.
And soon, he was drafted out with drums and cheers.

Some cheered him home, but not as crowds cheer Goal.
Only a solemn man who brought him fruits
Thanked him; and then inquired about his soul.
Now, he will spend a few sick years in Institutes,
And do what things the rules consider wise,   40
And take whatever pity they may dole.
To-night he noticed how the women's eyes
Passed from him to the strong men that were whole.
How cold and late it is! Why don't they come
And put him into bed? Why don't they come?

Wilfred Owen

Strange Hells

There are strange Hells within the minds War made
Not so often, not so humiliatingly afraid
As one would have expected – the racket and fear guns
    made.

One Hell the Gloucester soldiers they quite put out;
Their first bombardment, when in combined black
    shout
Of fury, guns aligned, they ducked lower their heads
And sang with diaphragms fixed beyond all dreads,
That tin and stretched-wire tinkle, that blither of tune;
'Après la guerre fini' till Hell all had come down,
Twelve-inch, six-inch, and eighteen-pounders
    hammering Hell's thunders.   10

Where are they now on State-doles, or showing shop-
    patterns
Or walking town to town sore in borrowed tatterns
Or begged. Some civic routine one never learns.
The heart burns – but has to keep out of face how
    heart burns.

Ivor Gurney

The Superfluous Woman

Ghosts crying down the vistas of the years,
Recalling words
Whose echoes long have died;
And kind moss grown
Over the sharp and blood-bespattered stones
Which cut our feet upon the ancient ways.

*

But who will look for my coming?

Long busy days where many meet and part;
Crowded aside
Remembered hours of hope;   10
And city streets
Grown dark and hot with eager multitudes
Hurrying homeward whither respite waits.

*

But who will seek me at nightfall?

Light fading where the chimneys cut the sky;
Footsteps that pass,
Nor tarry at my door.
And far away,
Behind the row of crosses, shadows black
Stretch out long arms before the smouldering sun.   20

*

But who will give me my children?

Vera Brittain

Men Fade Like Rocks

Rock-like the souls of men
    Fade, fade in time.
Falls on worn surfaces,
    Slow chime on chime,

Sense, like a murmuring dew,
    Soft sculpturing rain,
Or the wind that blows hollowing
    In every lane.

Smooth as the stones that lie
    Dimmed, water-worn,
Worn of the night and day,
    In sense forlorn,

Rock-like the souls of men
    Fade, fade in time;
Smoother than river-rain
    Falls chime on chime.

W. J. Turner

High Wood

Ladies and gentlemen, this is High Wood,
Called by the French, Bois des Fourneaux,
The famous spot which in Nineteen-Sixteen,
July, August and September was the scene
Of long and bitterly contested strife,
By reason of its High commanding site.
Observe the effects of shell-fire in the trees
Standing and fallen; here is wire; this trench
For months inhabited, twelve times changed hands;
(They soon fall in), used later as a grave.   10
It has been said on good authority
That in the fighting for this patch of wood
Were killed somewhere above eight thousand men,
Of whom the greater part were buried here,
This mound on which you stand being . . .
                          Madam, please,
You are requested kindly not to touch
Or take away the Company's property
As souvenirs; you'll find we have on sale
A large variety, all guaranteed.   20
As I was saying, all is as it was,
This is an unknown British officer,
The tunic having lately rotted off.
Please follow me – this way . . .
                      the *path*, sir, *please*,
The ground which was secured at great expense
The Company keeps absolutely untouched,

And in that dug-out (genuine) we provide
Refreshments at a reasonable rate.
You are requested not to leave about   30
Paper, or ginger-beer bottles, or orange peel,
There are waste-paper-baskets at the gate.

Philip Johnstone

Picture-Show

And still they come and go: and this is all I know –
That from the gloom I watch an endless picture-show,
Where wild or listless faces flicker on their way,
With glad or grievous hearts I'll never understand
Because Time spins so fast, and they've no time to stay
Beyond the moment's gesture of a lifted hand.

And still, between the shadow and the blinding flame,
The brave despair of men flings onward, ever the same
As in those doom-lit years that wait them, and have
    been . . .
And life is just the picture dancing on a screen.   10

Siegfried Sassoon

Festubert, 1916

Tired with dull grief, grown old before my day,
I sit in solitude and only hear
Long silent laughters, murmurings of dismay,
The lost intensities of hope and fear;
In those old marshes yet the rifles lie,
On the thin breastwork flutter the grey rags,
The very books I read are there – and I
Dead as the men I loved, wait while life drags

Its wounded length from those sad streets of war
Into green places here, that were my own;   10
But now what once was mine is mine no more,
I seek such neighbours here and I find none.
With such strong gentleness and tireless will
Those ruined houses seared themselves in me,
Passionate I look for their dumb story still,
And the charred stub outspeaks the living tree.

I rise up at the singing of a bird
And scarcely knowing slink along the lane,
I dare not give a soul a look or word
Where all have homes and none's at home in vain: 20
Deep red the rose burned in the grim redoubt,
The self-sown wheat around was like a flood,
In the hot path the lizard lolled time out,
The saints in broken shrines were bright as blood.

Sweet Mary's shrine between the sycamores!
There we would go, my friend of friends and I,

And snatch long moments from the grudging wars;
Whose dark made light intense to see them by . . .
Shrewd bit the morning fog, the whining shots
Spun from the wrangling wire; then in warm swoon   30
The sun hushed all but the cool orchard plots,
We crept in the tall grass and slept till noon.

Edmund Blunden

Lamplight

We planned to shake the world together, you and I
Being young, and very wise;
Now in the light of the green shaded lamp
Almost I see your eyes
Light with the old gay laughter; you and I
Dreamed greatly of an Empire in those days,
Setting our feet upon laborious ways,
And all you asked of fame
Was crossed swords in the Army List,
My Dear, against your name.   10

We planned a great Empire together, you and I,
Bound only by the sea;
Now in the quiet of a chill Winter's night
Your voice comes hushed to me
Full of forgotten memories: you and I
Dreamed great dreams of our future in those days,
Setting our feet on undiscovered ways,
And all I asked of fame
A scarlet cross on my breast, my Dear,
For the swords by your name.   20

We shall never shake the world together, you and I,
For you gave your life away;
And I think my heart was broken by the war,
Since on a summer day
You took the road we never spoke of: you and I
Dreamed greatly of an Empire in those days;
You set your feet upon the Western ways

And have no need of fame –
There's a scarlet cross on my breast, my Dear,
And a torn cross with your name. 30

May Wedderburn Cannan

Recalling War

Entrance and exit wounds are silvered clean,
The track aches only when the rain reminds.
The one-legged man forgets his leg of wood,
The one-armed man his jointed wooden arm.
The blinded man sees with his ears and hands
As much or more than once with both his eyes.
Their war was fought these twenty years ago
And now assumes the nature-look of time,
As when the morning traveller turns and views
His wild night-stumbling carved into a hill.   10

What, then, was war? No mere discord of flags
But an infection of the common sky
That sagged ominously upon the earth
Even when the season was the airiest May.
Down pressed the sky, and we, oppressed, thrust out
Boastful tongue, clenched fist and valiant yard.
Natural infirmities were out of mode,
For Death was young again: patron alone
Of healthy dying, premature fate-spasm.

Fear made fine bed-fellows. Sick with delight   20
At life's discovered transitoriness,
Our youth became all-flesh and waived the mind.
Never was such antiqueness of romance,
Such tasty honey oozing from the heart.
And old importances came swimming back –
Wine, meat, log-fires, a roof over the head,
A weapon at the thigh, surgeons at call.

Even there was a use again for God –
A word of rage in lack of meat, wine, fire,
In ache of wounds beyond all surgeoning.   30

War was return of earth to ugly earth,
War was foundering of sublimities,
Extinction of each happy art and faith
By which the world had still kept head in air.
Protesting logic or protesting love,
Until the unendurable moment struck –
The inward scream, the duty to run mad.

And we recall the merry ways of guns –
Nibbling the walls of factory and church
Like a child, piecrust; felling groves of trees   40
Like a child, dandelions with a switch.
Machine-guns rattle toy-like from a hill,
Down in a row the brave tin-soldiers fall:
A sight to be recalled in elder days
When learnedly the future we devote
To yet more boastful visions of despair.

Robert Graves

War Books

What did they expect of our toil and extreme
Hunger – the perfect drawing of a heart's dream?
Did they look for a book of wrought art's perfection,
Who promised no reading, nor praise, nor publication?
Out of the heart's sickness the spirit wrote
For delight, or to escape hunger, or of war's worst
    anger,
When the guns died to silence, and men would gather
    sense
Somehow together, and find this was life indeed,
And praise another's nobleness, or to Cotswold get
    hence.
There we wrote – Corbie Ridge – or in Gonnehem
    at rest.   10
Or Fauquissart or world's death songs, ever the best.
One made sorrows' praise passing the church where
    silence
Opened for the long quivering strokes of the bell –
Another wrote all soldiers' praise, and of France and
    night's stars.
Served his guns, got immortality, and died well.
But Ypres played another trick with its danger on me,
Kept still the needing and loving of action body;
Gave no candles, and nearly killed me twice as well,
And no souvenirs though I risked my life in the stuck
    tanks,

Yet there was praise of Ypres, love came sweet in
    hospital   20
And old Flanders went under to long ages of plays
    thought in my pages.

Ivor Gurney

Aftermath

Have you forgotten yet? . . .
For the world's events have rumbled on since those
    gagged days,
Like traffic checked while at the crossing of city-ways:
And the haunted gap in your mind has filled with
    thoughts that flow
Like clouds in the lit heaven of life; and you're a man
    reprieved to go,
Taking your peaceful share of Time, with joy to spare.
*But the past is just the same – and War's a bloody
    game . . .*
Have you forgotten yet? . . .
*Look down, and swear by the slain of the War that
    you'll never forget.*

Do you remember the dark months you held the
    sector at Mametz –   10
The nights you watched and wired and dug and piled
    sandbags on parapets?
Do you remember the rats; and the stench
Of corpses rotting in front of the front-line trench –
And dawn coming, dirty-white, and chill with a
    hopeless rain?
Do you ever stop and ask, 'Is it all going to happen
    again?'

Do you remember that hour of din before the attack –
And the anger, the blind compassion that seized and
    shook you then

As you peered at the doomed and haggard faces of
   your men?
Do you remember the stretcher-cases lurching back
With dying eyes and lolling heads – those
   ashen-grey   20
Masks of the lads who once were keen and kind and
   gay?

Have you forgotten yet? . . .
Look up, and swear by the green of the spring that
   you'll never forget.

Siegfried Sassoon

If ye Forget

Let me forget – Let me forget,
I am weary of remembrance,
And my brow is ever wet,
With the tears of my remembrance,
With the tears and bloody sweat,
   Let me forget.

If ye forget – If ye forget,
Then your children must remember,
And their brow be ever wet,
With the tears of their remembrance,   10
With the tears and bloody sweat,
   If ye forget.

G. A. Studdert Kennedy

The Midnight Skaters

The hop-poles stand in cones,
   The icy pond lurks under,
The pole-tops touch the star-gods' thrones
   And sound the gulfs of wonder,
But not the tallest there, 'tis said,
Could fathom to this pond's black bed.

Then is not death at watch
   Within those secret waters?
What wants he but to catch
   Earth's heedless sons and daughters?   10
With but a crystal parapet
Between, he has his engines set.

Then on, blood shouts, on, on,
   Twirl, wheel and whip above him,
Dance on this ball-floor thin and wan,
   Use him as though you love him;
Court him, elude him, reel and pass,
And let him hate you through the glass.

Edmund Blunden

Ancient History

Adam, a brown old vulture in the rain,
Shivered below his wind-whipped olive-trees;
Huddling sharp chin on scarred and scraggy knees,
He moaned and mumbled to his darkening brain;
'He was the grandest of them all – was Cain!
A lion laired in the hills, that none could tire;
Swift as a stag; a stallion of the plain,
Hungry and fierce with deeds of huge desire.'

Grimly he thought of Abel, soft and fair –
A lover with disaster in his face,   10
And scarlet blossom twisted in bright hair.
'Afraid to fight; was murder more disgrace? . . .
God always hated Cain.' . . . He bowed his head –
The gaunt wild man whose lovely sons were dead.

Siegfried Sassoon

The Next War

The long war had ended.
Its miseries had grown faded.
Deaf men became difficult to talk to.
Heroes became bores.

Those alchemists
Who had converted blood into gold,
Had grown elderly.
But they held a meeting,
Saying,
'We think perhaps we ought   10
To put up tombs
Or erect altars
To those brave lads
Who were so willingly burnt,
Or blinded,
Or maimed,
Who lost all likeness to a living thing,
Or were blown to bleeding patches of flesh
For our sakes.
It would look well.   20
Or we might even educate the children.'

But the richest of these wizards
Coughed gently;
And he said,
'I have always been to the front
– In private enterprise –
I yield in public spirit

272

To no man.
I think yours is a very good idea
– A capital idea –   30
And not too costly.
But it seems to me
That the cause for which we fought
Is again endangered.
What more fitting memorial for the fallen
Than that their children
Should fall for the same cause?'
Rushing eagerly into the street,
The kindly old gentlemen cried
To the young: 40
    'Will you sacrifice
    Through your lethargy
    What your fathers died to gain?
    Our cause is in peril.
    The world must be made safe for the young!'
And the children
Went . . .

Osbert Sitwell

The War Generation: Ave

In cities and in hamlets we were born,
    And little towns behind the van of time;
A closing era mocked our guileless dawn
    With jingles of a military rhyme.
But in that song we heard no warning chime,
    Nor visualised in hours benign and sweet
The threatening woe that our adventurous feet
    Would starkly meet.

Thus we began, amid the echoes blown
    Across our childhood from an earlier war,   10
Too dim, too soon forgotten, to dethrone
    Those dreams of happiness we thought secure;
While, imminent and fierce outside the door,
    Watching a generation grow to flower,
The fate that held our youth within its power
    Waited its hour.

Vera Brittain

To a Conscript of 1940

*Qui n'a pas une fois désespéré de l'honneur,
ne sera jamais un héros.*
Georges Bernanos

A soldier passed me in the freshly fallen snow,
   His footsteps muffled, his face unearthly grey;
And my heart gave a sudden leap
   As I gazed on a ghost of five-and-twenty years ago.

I shouted Halt! and my voice had the old accustomed
      ring
   And he obeyed it as it was obeyed
In the shrouded days when I too was one
   Of an army of young men marching

Into the unknown. He turned towards me and I said:
   'I am one of those who went before you   10
Five-and-twenty years ago: one of the many who never
      returned,
   Of the many who returned and yet were dead.

We went where you are going, into the rain and the
      mud;
   We fought as you will fight
With death and darkness and despair;
   We gave what you will give – our brains and our
      blood.

We think we gave in vain. The world was not renewed.
　　There was hope in the homestead and anger in the
　　　　streets
But the old world was restored and we returned
　　To the dreary field and workshop, and the
　　　　immemorial feud　　　　　　　　　　　　　　　20

Of rich and poor. Our victory was our defeat.
　　Power was retained where power had been misused
And youth was left to sweep away
　　The ashes that the fires had strewn beneath our feet.

But one thing we learned: there is no glory in the deed
　　Until the soldier wears a badge of tarnished braid;
There are heroes who have heard the rally and have
　　　　seen
　　The glitter of a garland round their head.

Theirs is the hollow victory. They are deceived.
　　But you, my brother and my ghost, if you can go　　30
Knowing that there is no reward, no certain use
　　In all your sacrifice, then honour is reprieved.

To fight without hope is to fight with grace,
　　The self reconstructed, the false heart repaired.'
Then I turned with a smile, and he answered my salute
　　As he stood against the fretted hedge, which was like
　　　　white lace.

Herbert Read

CODA

Ancre Sunshine

In all his glory the sun was high and glowing
Over the farm world where we found great peace,
And clearest blue the winding river flowing
Seemed to be celebrating a release
From all but speed and music of its own
Which but for some few cows we heard alone.

Here half a century before might I,
Had something chanced, about this point have lain,
Looking with failing sense on such blue sky,
And then become a name with others slain.   10
But that thought vanished. Claire was wandering free
Miraumont way in the golden tasselled lea.

The railway trains went by, and dreamily
I thought of them as planets in their course,
Though bound perhaps for Arras, how would we
Have wondered once if through the furious force
Murdering our world one of these same had come,
Friendly and sensible – 'the war's over, chum'.

And now it seemed Claire was afar, and I
Alone, and where she went perhaps the mill   20
That used to be had risen again, and by
All that had fallen was in its old form still,

For her to witness, with no cold surprise,
In one of those moments when nothing dies.

Edmund Blunden

Notes

Military terms, soldiers' slang and place names are explained in the glossary rather than in the notes on individual poems.

Prelude: 'On the idle hill of summer'

fife: A wind instrument associated with military music since the early 1500s, when Swiss troops used both fifes and drums for signalling purposes in battle.

files of scarlet: Line regiments in the British army wore a red jacket until the late 1880s, when khaki became the standard colour.

1 YOUR COUNTRY NEEDS YOU
'Let the foul Scene proceed'

Channel Firing

This prophetic poem is dated 'April, 1914'.

chancel: The part of a church containing the altar and seats for the clergy and choir.

Judgement-day: The end of the world, when God returns to judge all mankind: 'Every idle word that men shall speak, they shall give account thereof in the day of judgement' (Matthew 12:36).

glebe-cow: A glebe is a plot of land belonging to an English parish church.

Mad as hatters: A reference to the Mad Hatter in Lewis Carroll's *Alice in Wonderland* (1865). The nineteenth-century hat-making industry used mercury in its processes, and prolonged exposure to this caused hatters to suffer from such symptoms as trembling, slurred speech, memory loss and depression.

Parson Thirdly: A character in Hardy's novel *Far from the Madding Crowd* (1874).

Stourton Tower: This tower was built in Wiltshire in 1772 to commemorate King Alfred's victory over the Saxons in 879.

Camelot: The legendary site of King Arthur's palace and court has tentatively been located at Cadbury Castle in Somerset.

Stonehenge: A circle of prehistoric megaliths on Salisbury Plain in Wiltshire.

The Eve of War

the Circus: Probably Piccadilly Circus, a busy junction in central London.

the staring arc: An illuminated advertising hoarding.

The Marionettes

Marionettes: Puppets moved from above by the manipulation of wires.

upsweal: Rise.

August, 1914

stooks: Cut sheaves of hay, traditionally stacked in pyramid-shaped clusters in fields at the end of summer.

covey: The collective name for a group of partridges.

fold: An enclosure for livestock, especially sheep.

wold: An area of high, open uncultivated land.

rout: A disorderly or tumultuous crowd.

tilted stacks: Haystacks.

fallow: A ploughed area of farmland left unsown for a period of time.

loam: Soil consisting of varying proportions of clay, silt, and sand.

Downs: The Berkshire Downs are part of a picturesque area of gently hilly countryside in southern England to the west of London.

byres: Cow sheds.

brae: A hillside especially alongside a river, and also a colloquialism meaning 'raw or fierce weather'.

Happy is England Now

the destroying Dragon: England's patron saint is St George, who killed a dragon that was laying waste to the countryside.

This is no case of petty Right or Wrong

The phoenix: A mythical Egyptian bird said to die on a funeral pyre and to rise again from the ashes.

made us from dust: An echo of Genesis 2:7, where God creates Adam from 'the dust of the ground'.

The Poets are Waiting

fashion-plate: Fashion magazines at this time frequently contained glossy pages or plates illustrating the most up-to-date and stylish clothing.

Plated and mailed: Wearing body armour. Chain mail is constructed from interlocked rings of metal, and plate mail consists of welded plates of metal.

The Dilemma

'Gott strafe England': German for 'God Punish England', a slogan frequently used in early German wartime propaganda.

'Who's for the khaki suit'

The Call

French: Sir John French (1852–1925) was Commander-in-Chief
   of the British Expeditionary Force between August 1914 and
   December 1915.

Recruiting

'Lads, you're wanted, go and help': This slogan appears to be
   Mackintosh's own invention, but it echoes many posters of
   the time encouraging enlistment. They bore slogans such as
   'Is Your Best Boy in Khaki?' and 'There's Room for You!
   Enlist To-Day'.
Girls with feathers: In the early months of the war, organiza-
   tions such as The Order of The White Feather gave men not
   in uniforms white feathers, meant to represent cowardice, but
   the practice proved highly unpopular and was soon stopped.
Washy: Slang for 'lacking in strength or character'.
three score and ten: Seventy: 'The days of our years are three-
   score years and ten; and if by reason of strength they be
   fourscore years, yet is their strength labour and sorrow; for
   it is soon cut off, and we fly away' (Psalms 90:10).

Soldier: Twentieth Century

Titan: In Greek mythology, the Titans were pre-Olympian gods
   or demi-gods, the children of Uranus and capable of enor-
   mous power and strength.
Napoleon: Napoleon Bonaparte (1769–1821) became commander
   of the French army in 1796 and was emperor of France
   between 1804 and 1814. He emerged from exile to be defeated
   at the Battle of Waterloo in 1815.
Caesar: Julius Caesar (*c.* 101–44 BC) invaded Britain in 55 BC.

He became a dictator in Rome, and founded the Julian dynasty of emperors.

Circe's swine: In Book 10 of Homer's *Odyssey*, Odysseus' men are turned into pigs by the sorceress Circe while sleeping on the island of Aeaea.

Youth in Arms I

David: The Jewish Old Testament king famed for his defeat of the Philistine Goliath in his youth: 'And David put his hand in his bag, and took thence a stone, and slang it, and smote the Philistine in his forehead, that the stone sunk into his forehead; and he fell upon his face to the earth' (1 Samuel 17:49). His subsequent military victories were envied by his adoptive father, Saul, who subsequently plotted to kill him. 'And the women answered one another as they played, and said, Saul hath slain his thousands, and David his ten thousands' (1 Samuel 18:7).

avatar: Incarnation or manifestation.

Greybeards: Old men.

baize: Green felted wool cloth often used to cover gaming tables.

'I don't want to be a soldier'

Sung to the tune of 'On Sunday I Walk Out With a Soldier', from the popular revue *The Passing Show of 1914*.

The Conscript

thorn-crowned head, | The nail-marks: A crown of thorns, a mock symbol of royalty, was forced upon Jesus before his crucifixion, according to Matthew 27:29, Mark 15:17 and John 19:2.

Rondeau of a Conscientious Objector

Rondeau: A medieval French verse form consisting of thirteen octosyllabic lines grouped into stanzas of five, three and five lines. The rondeau uses only two rhymes, and the first word or phrase of the first line recurs twice as a refrain after the second and third stanzas. Technically Lawrence's poem is not a rondeau.

conscientious objector: A person who, for political, moral or religious reasons, refused to fight during the war.

In Training

The Kiss

Brother Lead: A bullet.
Sister Steel: The bayonet.

Arms and the Boy

Arms and the Boy: The title is probably an allusion either to George Bernard Shaw's anti-romantic drama about militarism, *Arms and the Man* (1894), or to Siegfried Sassoon's poem 'Arms and the Man', first published in *The Old Huntsman and Other Poems* (1917). Both works derive their title from the opening line of John Dryden's 1697 translation of the *Aeneid*, the epic poem by the Roman poet Virgil (70–19 BC): 'Arms, and the man I sing.'

For his teeth . . . his curls: The creature referred to in the third stanza does not seem to be based on any recognizable mythological animal or figure, and could be either a generic form of devil or merely a product of Owen's imagination.

'All the hills and vales along'

Barabbas: Pontius Pilate, the Roman governor in Jerusalem, set free the thief Barabbas in preference to Jesus at the Feast of the Passover (John 18:38–40).

Hemlock: A white flowering plant known for its poisonous qualities.

Socrates: A Greek philosopher (470–399 BC), who was found guilty of corrupting the young and was forced to kill himself by drinking hemlock.

'We are Fred Karno's army'

Sung to the tune of the hymn 'The Church's One Foundation', by Samuel J. Stone and Samuel Sebastian Wesley.

Fred Karno: The stage name of Fred Wescott (1866–1941), a knock-about music-hall comedian, often used to describe a muddle.

ragtime: A popular form of music-hall entertainment, of African-American origin.

Hoch! Hoch! Mein Gott: German, literally meaning 'High! High! My God'.

Song of the Dark Ages

down: A gently rolling hill.

barrows: Grave mounds or tumuli.

calcined: Reduced to quicklime, desiccated or burnt to ashes.

ossuary: A depository for the bones of the dead.

sod: A piece of turf.

Sonnets 1917: Servitude

This is the third of a group of five sonnets which Gurney dedicated 'To the Memory of Rupert Brooke'. He described them in a letter of 14 February 1917 as 'a sort of counterblast against "Sonnetts 1914" [*sic*], which were written by an officer . . . They are the protest of the physical against the exulted spiritual; of the cumulative weighted small facts against the one large. Of informed opinion against uninformed.'

In Barracks

soldiers of the Line: Members of a regular army regiment, as opposed to those regiments which were raised specially from civilian volunteers during the First World War.

'Men Who March Away'

purblind: Lacking in vision, insight, or understanding.
Dalliers: People who dawdle or take things slowly.
braggarts: Boastful people.

Marching Men

Calvary: The hill upon which Christ was crucified.
Seven swords: A conflation of the seven wounds inflicted on Christ at his crucifixion and the seven sorrows of his mother Mary, a series of religious observances instigated in the thirteenth century.
rent: Torn.

Fragment

pashed: Smashed.
phosphorus: A substance that shines or glows green in the dark, often noticed on breaking waves at sea.

2 SOMEWHERE IN FRANCE
In Trenches

First Time In

Oilsheets: Pieces of canvas impregnated with oil to make them waterproof, used to cover dugouts.
Ulysses: In Greek mythology, Odysseus – known as Ulysses in Latin – blinded the Cyclops Polyphemus after the Trojan Wars

and was cursed by the god Poseidon never to reach home. The goddess Athena intervened, and after ten years Ulysses returned to his family in Ithaca.

'David of the White Rock': Sometimes known by its Welsh title, 'Dafydd y Garreg Wen', this folk song was highly popular among Welsh soldiers.

'Slumber Song': Probably the traditional Welsh lullaby 'All Through the Night', which talks of how 'Soft the drowsy hours are creeping | Hill and vale in slumber sleeping'.

Beautiful tune . . . roguish words: Gurney may have in mind one of the mildly obscene versions of the Salvation Army hymn 'Wash Me in the Water' popular during the war, or perhaps 'Big Willie's Luvly Daughter', a variant of 'Where are the Boys of the Village Tonight' favoured by the Welsh Fusiliers which, according to David Jones in his notes to Part V of *In Parenthesis* (London: Faber & Faber, 1938), suggested that 'the object of the British Expedition into France was to enjoy the charms of the Emperor's daughter'.

Break of Day in the Trenches

druid: A pre-Christian Celtic priest.

poppy: The red poppy (*Papaver rhoeas*) flourishes in disturbed ground and was a ubiquitous sight on the Western Front. The practice of selling artificial poppies to raise money for wounded ex-servicemen immediately after the war resulted in it becoming an internationally recognized symbol of remembrance.

'Bombed last night'

Sung to the tune of the music-hall song 'Drunk Last Night and Drunk the Night Before'.

Higher Germany: An allusion to the traditional English folk song

'High Germany', which describes a lover going off to fight in the wars between England and France of 1702 to 1713.

Breakfast

Hull United: No football team with that name existed in 1914 when the poem was written; like *Jimmy Stainthorp* and *Billy Bradford*, it seems to be Gibson's own invention. However, Hull City Reserves and Halifax Town both played in the Midland Counties League and met twice in 1914 – on 3 October and 12 November – so one of these matches may be what Gibson has in mind.

In the Trenches

Demeter: The Greek corn goddess, whose search for her daughter Persephone took her into the underworld.

Psyche: In Greek mythology, the woman so beautiful that men would worship her instead of courting her. Aphrodite, the goddess of love, was jealous and sent her son Eros to make Psyche fall in love with an unworthy man, but he fell in love with her himself. After several complications, the two eventually united. *Psyche* is also the Greek for 'soul'.

Pleiades: Also known as the Seven Sisters, in Greek mythology these were the daughters of the demi-god Atlas and were nymphs in the train of the goddess Artemis. They were eventually placed in the sky, where they form one of the most visible constellations of stars in the northern hemisphere.

Orion swings his belt: In Greek mythology, Orion the hunter was unwittingly killed by the goddess Artemis, who, in remorse, placed him in the sky as a constellation of stars; three parallel stars in the middle of the constellation represent his belt.

carrion crow: A common black crow which feeds on rotten flesh (carrion).

Winter Warfare

Tabs: Senior officers in the British army wore red tabs on their lapels.

rime: The frost caused by a sudden and rapid drop in temperature.

spurs: Worn by senior officers as well as cavalry in the British army.

hoary: Grey or white with age, or with a kind of frost.

Hauptman Kälte: German for 'Captain Cold'. ('Hauptman' is more usually spelled 'Hauptmann'.)

Futility

clays: A poeticism for 'mankind', possibly echoing Genesis 2:7, where God creates Adam from 'the dust of the ground', or John Milton's *Paradise Lost* (1667): 'Did I request thee, Maker, from my clay | To mould me man?' (X, 743–4).

cold star: The Earth.

fatuous: Foolish and pointless.

Exposure

glozed: Shining brightly.

'We're here because we're here'

Sung to the tune of 'Auld Lang Syne'.

Poem: Abbreviated from the Conversation of Mr. T. E. H.

Frequently credited to the philosopher and poet T. E. Hulme (1883–1917), this poem has a somewhat confusing history. It first appeared in Pound's periodical *Catholic Anthology* in

November 1915 under Hulme's name. When Pound included 'The Complete Poetical Works of T. E. Hulme' as an appendix to his collection *Umbra* (1920), he added the note 'Hulme's five poems were published as his *Complete Poetical Works* at the end of *Ripostes*, in 1912; there is, and now can be, no further addition, unless my abbreviation of some of his talk made when he came home with his first wound in 1915 may be half counted among them.' On this evidence, the poem has been credited to Pound.

Piccadilly: A busy thoroughfare in central London.

Illusions

gloze: Insert an explanation or comment upon.
nemesis: An agent of retribution and downfall.
malkins: Scarecrows, ragged puppets or grotesque effigies.

The Silent One

Bucks: Buckinghamshire.
stripes: Embroidered cloth chevrons worn on the upper sleeve to denote rank. In the British army, a lance corporal wears one stripe, a full corporal wears two, and a sergeant wears three.
finicking: Excessively fussy or exacting.

Moonrise over Battlefield

fard: Cosmetics.
punk: Prostitute.
white-shirted: German shock troops wore white overshirts as camouflage during the winter.

The Redeemer

lugged: Slang for 'carried or dragged with difficulty'.
mirk: Murk, gloom.

thorny crown: The mock symbol of royalty forced upon Jesus before his crucifixion, according to Matthew 27:29, Mark 15:17 and John 19:2.

Lancaster on Lune: The river Lune flows through the northern town of Lancaster.

Serenade

Schubert: Franz Schubert (1797–1828), the Austrian classical composer, whose instrumental works combine a classical heritage with nineteenth-century romanticism.

'Heldenleben': Literally meaning 'A Hero's Life', the symphonic poem *Ein Heldenleben* by Richard Strauss (1864–1949) was first performed in 1898.

'wir haben | Sich geliebt': Gurney's German seems to be faulty here; he has written 'we loved ourselves', whereas the context suggests that he meant to write 'we have such love'.

Behind the Lines

Grotesque

Dante: Dante Alighieri (1265–1321), the Italian poet, philosopher and author of *La Divina Commedia* (*c.* 1314–21), which describes his journey into hell through seven circles of sin.

Louse Hunting

Gargantuan: According to the French humanist and satirical author François Rabelais (*c.* 1494–*c.* 1553) in his *Gargantua and Pantagruel* (1532–52), Gargantua was a giant known for his voracious hunger and who ate his nursemaid.

smutch: An archaic variant for 'smudge'.

Highland fling: The traditional Scottish dance which involves vigorous whirling and raising the arms above the head.

revel: A riotous celebration.

At Senlis Once

cataract: A large waterfall descending steeply or in steps.
mill-sails: Blades attached to the arms of a windmill.
an honest glass: The correct measure of an alcoholic drink.
pierrots: In French pantomime, Pierrot is a lovesick clown who
    wears a frilled, spotty shirt and has a whitened, tear-stained
    face. 'Pierrot' was the generic name for comic performers in
    music halls.

Crucifix Corner

chlorinated: Chlorine was used as a water-purifier on the Western
    Front.
Noel: Christmas.
new term: The spring term of the academic year begins in January.
Severn: A river that rises in Wales and runs through
    Gloucestershire.
last Trump: The trumpet call that will awaken the dead at the
    end of the world: 'In a moment, in the twinkling of an eye,
    at the last trump . . . the trumpet shall sound and the dead
    shall be raised incorruptible, and we shall be changed' (1
    Corinthians 15:52).
'Hundred Pipers and A': A traditional Scots song, with modern
    words by Lady Nairne (1766–1845), used as a marching song
    by Scottish regiments.
'Happy we've been a'together': A sentimental Scottish folk
    song popular among Highland regiments during the Great
    War.
leavens: Agencies which have a transforming effect from
    within.

Vlamertinghe: Passing the Chateau, July, 1917

'And all her silken flanks with garlands drest': A quotation from 'Ode on a Grecian Urn' by John Keats (1795–1821), first published in *Lamia, Isabella, The Eve of St Agnes, and Other Poems* (1820).

poppies: The red poppy (*Papaver rhoeas*) flourishes in disturbed ground and was a ubiquitous sight on the Western Front. The practice of selling artificial poppies to raise money for wounded ex-servicemen immediately after the war resulted in it becoming an internationally recognized symbol of remembrance.

damask: A reversible lustrous fabric and the cloth used to make Roman emperors' robes.

vermilion: A rich purple-red colour. In Roman society, the only citizen allowed to wear purple was the emperor.

Dead Cow Farm

An ancient saga: Snorri Sturluson's *Edda* (*c.* 1220), a textbook of Norse poetry, which tells how the cow Auðumla created the first man, Búri, by licking salty blocks of ice.

The Sower

wain: An archaism for a heavy wagon used in farming.

August, 1918

shoon: An archaism for 'shoes'.

'Therefore is the name of it called Babel'

'Therefore . . . Babel': See 'Therefore is the name of it called Babel; because the Lord did there confound the language of all the earth: and from thence did the Lord scatter them abroad upon the face of all the earth' (Genesis 11:9). The

Tower of Babel was built by mankind to reach heaven. God was angered by this arrogance, and divided the people by scattering them over the face of the earth and giving them different languages.

lees: Dregs at the bottom of a bottle or glass.

Comrades of War

Canadians

Canadians: Approximately 600,000 Canadian soldiers fought in the First World War, of whom 210,100 were wounded, captured or killed.

Saskatchewan: A central western state in Canada.

Ontario: A central state in Canada.

Jack London: An American novelist and travel writer (1876–1916), best known for *The Call of the Wild* (1903), *White Fang* (1906) and *John Barleycorn* (1913).

Woodbine Willie

Woodbine Willie: Studdert Kennedy was nicknamed 'Woodbine Willie' by the troops, because of his practice of supplying them with plentiful cigarettes, including the Woodbine brand.

Apologia pro Poemate Meo

Apologia pro Poemate Meo: Latin for 'Apology for my poetry'.

Seraphic: Belonging to the highest order of angels.

spate: A sudden flood.

My Company

Foule! . . . mon corps: French for 'Horde! Your entire soul is standing upright in my body'.

Jules Romains: The French writer and playwright (1885–1972) of largely philosophical texts and the chief exponent of Unanimism, a literary theory positing a collective spirit or personality.

Samoa: A group of islands in the Pacific Ocean, about 2,700 kilometres north-east of New Zealand. According to Robert Louis Stevenson in Chapter V of *In the South Seas* (1888), 'Samoans are the most chaste of Polynesians, and they are to this day entirely fertile; Marquesans are the most debauched.' Later, however, he alludes to 'the story of the discovery of Tutuila, when the really decent women of Samoa prostituted themselves in public to the French'.

Before the Battle

jet: A black semi-precious stone.

numbered down, formed fours: This refers to the military practice whereby soldiers number themselves off in fours and then line up four abreast, usually before marching.

Greater Love

Greater Love: See John 15:13: 'Greater love hath no man than this, that a man lay down his life for his friends.'

lure: A contraction of 'allure'.

In Memoriam Private D. Sutherland . . .

In Memoriam: Latin for 'in memory of'.

To his Love

quick: Alive. See 'Who shall give account to him that is ready to judge the quick and the dead' (1 Peter 4:5).

Severn: A river that rises in Wales and runs through Gloucestershire.

Trench Poets

Donne: John Donne (1572–1631), the metaphysical poet and churchman, was dean of St Paul's Cathedral from 1621 and is best known for his religious and erotic poems and sermons.

'Get with child a mandrake-root': A quotation from Donne's 'Song' ('Goe and catche a falling starre'). The mandrake is a plant belonging to the potato family, the root of which is thought to resemble a man. It is considered a symbol of fertility and virility, although it is also a soporific. In the Bible, Rachel uses mandrake to promote conception (Genesis 30:14–15).

'I long to talk with some old lover's ghost': A quotation from Donne's 'Loves deitie', which, like 'Goe and catche a falling starre', was first published in *Poems, by J. D. With elegies on the authors death* (1633).

the Elegies: Fifteen poems by Donne, almost all written in the 1590s, that take the Roman poet Ovid (43 BC–AD 18) as their principal model and resemble his poems in ingenious wit and frank and unapologetic eroticism.

'What needst thou have more covering than a man': From Donne's 'Elegie XIX: To his Mistris going to Bed'.

Maud: A lengthy experimental poem by Alfred, Lord Tennyson (1809–92), first published in 1855. According to his son Hallam, in Chapter XIX of his *Alfred Lord Tennyson: A Memoir* (1897), Tennyson described the poem as 'a little Hamlet, the history of a morbid poetic soul under the blighting influence of a recklessly speculative age'. The poem ends with the narrator redeeming himself in the Crimean War.

3 ACTION
Rendezvous with Death

Before Action

benison: A blessing.

Into Battle

Dog-Star: Sirius, the brightest star in the northern hemisphere, and known as the Dog Star as it is part of the constellation Canis Major, or the Big Dog.

Sisters Seven: A constellation. In Greek mythology the Seven Sisters were the daughters of the demi-god Atlas and were nymphs in the train of the goddess Artemis. They were eventually placed in the sky, where they form one of the most visible constellations of stars in the northern hemisphere.

Orion's Belt: In Greek mythology, Orion the hunter was unwittingly killed by the goddess Artemis, who, in remorse, placed him in the sky as a constellation of stars; three parallel stars in the middle of the constellation represent his belt.

Two Sonnets

This poem has a footnote: '12 June 1915'.
Hoary: Ancient or venerable.

'I tracked a dead man down a trench'

This poem has a footnote: 'Written in trenches by "Glencourse Wood", 19–20th April, 1915.' Glencourse Wood was five kilometres east of Ypres. It changed hands a number of times during the war and was finally taken by the Australians in September 1917.

Ballad of the Three Spectres

fleering: Mocking, grinning or grimacing.

The Question

Gey: Dialect for 'very'.
bumming: Dialect for 'making a buzzing noise'.
Doomsday: The end of the world, when God returns to judge all mankind: 'Every idle word that men shall speak, they shall give account thereof in the day of Judgement' (Matthew 12:36).

The Soldier Addresses His Body

Hippogriff: A mythical beast having the head, wings and front legs of a griffin (itself a mythical creature having the head and wings of an eagle and the body of a lion) and the back legs of a horse.
agate: A precious gem, composed of quartz and of various colours.
Wyvern: A mythical beast in the form of a serpentine dragon with wings, and with an eagle's talons on its feet.
kvass: A Russian alcoholic drink, brewed from rye bread or grains and sometimes flavoured with herbs or fruit.

The Day's March

grides: Grates.

Battle

Eve of Assault: Infantry Going Down to Trenches

Yorks and Lancs: The York and Lancaster Regiment numbered 57,000 men during the First World War, of whom seven in ten were either wounded or killed.

drubbing: Beating.
the 'Un: The Hun.

Headquarters

league: An archaic measure of distance of approximately five
 kilometres.
ranging: Used here to mean both 'wide-ranging' and 'within range'.

It's a Queer Time

Treasure Island: The protagonists' goal in the piratical yarn of
 the same name by Robert Louis Stevenson (1850–94),
 published in 1883 and set in Cornwall and the West Indies.
the Spice winds: A conflation of the Spice Islands and the trade
 winds. The Spice Islands include Malaysia and Indonesia; their
 production of spices meant that in the fifteenth and sixteenth
 centuries trade was highly sought with them. Trade winds are
 winds that blow regularly in one direction, found about 30°
 from the Equator.
ho, for the Red West: Sail off into the sunset.
'Fag!': A fag is a cheap cigarette, or a younger boy who acts as
 a servant to a more senior boy in British public schools.
sailor suit: Traditional dress for young boys in Victorian times.
Tipperary: 'It's a long way to Tipperary', by Jack Judge and
 Harry Williams, was a popular soldiers' song.
Hymn of Hate: An anti-British song composed by Ernst Lissauer,
 very popular in Germany throughout the war, whose aggres-
 sive message is best summed up by its closing lines: 'We have
 one foe, and one foe alone – England.'

The Face

wraith: The phantom or spectre of someone, which usually appears as a warning that that person's death is imminent or has just occurred.

Gethsemane

Gethsemane: The place where Jesus and his disciples spent the night before his crucifixion: 'Then cometh Jesus with them unto a place called Gethsemane, and saith unto the disciples, Sit ye here, while I go and pray yonder' (Matthew 26:36).

ship: Put on.

I prayed my cup might pass: See 'And he went a little further, and fell on his face, and prayed, saying, O my Father, if it be possible, let this cup pass from me: nevertheless not as I will, but as thou wilt' (Matthew 26:39). Jesus prayed in the garden of Gethsemane to be spared his coming ordeal ('this cup'), while the disciples he took with him fell asleep, allowing him to be captured.

Anthem for Doomed Youth

passing-bells: A passing bell is a bell rung immediately after a death to indicate the dead person's passing.

orisons: Prayers.

pall: A cloth used to cover a coffin or tomb.

drawing-down of blinds: Blinds and curtains were traditionally drawn when a funeral cortège passed a house or when there had been a death in the household.

Spring Offensive

begird: Prepare and strengthen.

drave: Drove.

Youth in Arms III: Retreat

the old song: The songs which punctuate this poem appear to be Monro's own invention.

Aftermath

Back to Rest

lees: Dregs at the bottom of a bottle or glass.

Dulce et Decorum est

Dulce et Decorum est: This Latin quote, given in full at the end of the poem, is from Horace (65–8 BC), *Odes* III.ii.13. Owen's translation of it, given in a letter to his mother of 16 October 1917, is 'It is sweet and meet to die for one's country.'

clumsy helmets: Gas masks, probably of the Phenate-Hexamine Goggle Helmet variety, which consisted of a felt hood with perspex eyepieces.

lime: Either quicklime, a white caustic substance obtained from heating limestone, or birdlime, which is a sticky substance spread on twigs to trap small birds.

cud: Partially digested food, brought back into the mouth from the stomach for further chewing.

Field Ambulance in Retreat

Via Dolorosa, Via Sacra: Latin for 'Dolorous Way, Sacred Way', the name traditionally given to the road along which Christ carried the cross. *Via Dolorosa* is also the name given to a series of pictures or tableaux representing scenes in the Passion of Christ usually ranged at intervals around the walls of a church, although sometimes they can be found in the open air, especially on roads leading to a church or shrine.

league: An archaic measure of distance of approximately five kilometres.

standards: Regimental banners.

Dead Man's Dump

crowns of thorns: A crown of thorns, a mock symbol of royalty, was forced upon Jesus before his crucifixion, according to Matthew 27:29, Mark 15:17 and John 19:2.

God-ancestralled essences: Life.

pyre: A heap of combustible material used for burning corpses.

ichor: The ethereal fluid supposed to flow like blood in the veins of the gods.

Youth in Arms IV: Carrion

Carrion: Rotten meat.

Soliloquy II

carrion: Rotten meat.

Goya: Francisco José Goya y Lucientes (1746–1828), the Spanish artist whose paintings, drawings and engravings reflected contemporary historical upheavals. His series 'The Disasters of War' (1810–11) was one of the earliest graphic depictions of war.

Angelo: Michelangelo (1475–1564), the Italian Renaissance artist famous for numerous paintings, sculptures and architectural projects, among which were the ceiling of the Sistine Chapel and the statue *David*.

Butchers and Tombs

Cotswold stone: A distinctive honey-coloured limestone.

the Gloucesters: Soldiers of the Gloucestershire Regiment, with which Gurney served.

A Private

bedmen: A variant of 'beadsmen', men who pray for the salvation of others.

The Volunteer

This poem was actually written before the war and was sent in 1913 to *The Spectator*, where it was kept on file. The war made it suddenly topical, so it appeared in the issue of 8 August 1914.

oriflamme: The sacred banner of St Denis, received by early French kings from the abbot of St Denis before they set off to go to war. Later it came to mean anything – material or ideal – serving as a rallying point in a struggle.

Agincourt: Henry V (1387–1422) invaded France on 13 August 1415 and went on to defeat the French at Agincourt on 25 October.

In Flanders Fields

poppies: The red poppy (*Papaver rhoeas*) flourishes in disturbed ground and was a ubiquitous sight on the Western Front. The practice of selling artificial poppies to raise money for wounded ex-servicemen immediately after the war resulted in it becoming an internationally recognized symbol of remembrance.

Strange Meeting

Titanic wars: In Greek mythology, the Titanomachia was the ten-year war waged by Zeus and the Olympian gods against his father, Cronos, and the Titans, who were demi-gods capable of enormous power and strength.

groined: Scooped out.

flues: Ventilation shafts.

citadels: Castles or fortresses.

parried: To parry is to block a sword or bayonet thrust with another weapon.

Prisoners

meed: A much deserved reward.

4 BLIGHTY
Going Back

'I want to go home'
There is some uncertainty about the tune of this song. Ivor Gurney gives a transcription in a letter of 22 June 1916 with the comment: 'a very popular song about here. Not a brave song, but brave men sing it.'

If We Return

Rondeau: A medieval French verse form consisting of thirteen octosyllabic lines grouped into stanzas of five, three and five lines. The rondeau uses only two rhymes, and the first word or phrase of the first line recurs twice as a refrain after the second and third stanzas.

Home Service

top-hole: A slang term for 'excellent'.

Sick Leave

watches: Fixed periods of duty, usually lasting four hours.

Girl to Soldier on Leave

Titan: In Greek mythology, the Titans were pre-Olympian gods or demi-gods, the children of Uranus and capable of enormous power and strength.

the son of Zeus: Zeus had many sons, but this is probably a reference to Hercules, who was famed for his strength and fighting prowess.

Prometheus: In Greek myth, Prometheus stole fire from the gods for the benefit of mankind and was punished by being chained to a rock where an eagle tore daily at his liver, the liver healing up again every night.

Babel-cities: According to the Bible, the Tower of Babel was built by mankind to reach heaven. God was angered by this arrogance, and divided the people by scattering them over the face of the earth and giving them different languages. 'Therefore is the name of it called Babel; because the Lord did there confound the language of all the earth: and from thence did the Lord scatter them abroad upon the face of all the earth' (Genesis 11:9).

gyves: Fetters or shackles.

Circe's swine: In Book 10 of Homer's *Odyssey*, Odysseus' men are turned into pigs by the sorceress Circe while sleeping on the island of Aeaea.

repine: Feel discontent.

The Pavement

drabs: Prostitutes.

Leicester Square: A large square in the centre of London, famous for its theatres and a haunt of pleasure-seekers.

hanger: A wood on the side of a steep hill or bank.

The Other War

'I wore a tunic'

Sung to the tune of the popular American wartime ballad 'I Wore a Tulip', by Jack Mahoney and Percy Wenrich.

'Blighters'

'Blighters': The title is a pun on the soldiers' term for home – Blighty – and the slang term for a contemptuous or irritating person.

the House: The theatre.

rag-time: A popular form of music-hall entertainment, of African-American origin.

'Home, Sweet Home': A song with words by John Howard Payne and music by Henry Rowley Bishop, first heard in London in Bishop's opera *Clari, the Maid of Milan* (1823).

Ragtime (Wilfrid Gibson)

Ragtime: A popular form of music-hall entertainment, of African-American origin.

limelit: Before the introduction of electricity the best way to produce intense white light was by heating a piece of lime in an oxy-hydrogen flame. Such 'limelights' were widely used in theatres.

Strand: A busy thoroughfare in central London.

Air-Raid

brake: A thicket or clump of bushes.

Zeppelins

Zeppelins: Named after their inventor, Count Ferdinand von Zeppelin (1838–1917), Zeppelins were large, rigid-framed steerable airships which were used for bombing raids on Britain for much of the war. The first raid took place on Great Yarmouth and King's Lynn in Norfolk on 19 January 1915, while the first raid on London took place on 31 May 1915 and killed twenty-eight people, injuring another sixty.

serried: Standing close together.
surplice: A religious gown.

'Education'

quick: Alive. See 'Who shall give account to him that is ready to judge the quick and the dead' (1 Peter 4:5).
prate: Talk or chatter idly.
Krupps: A well-known German family of armament manufacturers, whose name was frequently used to refer to their products.

Socks

20 plain . . . decrease: The knitting pattern described in italics in the poem is not actually possible. Knitting socks and other clothing was seen as a patriotic gesture during the war, although many soldiers' memoirs complain of the poor quality of the clothing received.

A War Film

Cinema footage of the Mons Retreat does not exist. Official films do make reference to Mons retrospectively, and there was a feature film released in 1922, *Mons* (Gaumont British Instructional), which was dramatized but used veterans as extras and real army uniforms and equipment.
Nine moons: Nine months.

The War Films

God on earth: Jesus, the son of God.
seven sins: The seven deadly sins are Anger, Covetousness, Envy, Gluttony, Lust, Pride and Sloth.
sorrows seven: The seven sorrows of Mary, Christ's mother.
wayworn: Worn or wearied by travel.

The Dancers

carrion-fly: Several species of fly are able to feed on rotten flesh (carrion), including the bluebottle and the greenbottle.

'I looked up from my writing'

inditing: Putting things into literary form.
tattle: Rapid, careless talk.

Picnic

hurt-berries: Another name for bilberries, which flourish best on high ground and grow in large amounts on the Surrey hills.
Hurt Wood: A wood located in Surrey, between Guildford and Dorking (like *Hurt Hill*).
downs: A series of gently rolling hills.

As the Team's Head-Brass

Team: A set of animals harnessed together.
Head-Brass: Decorative polished brass plates placed on a horse's girdle.
fallow: A ploughed area of farmland left unsown for a period of time.
charlock: Wild mustard.
share: The blade of a plough.

The Farmer, 1917

cinctures: Girdles, or things which encircle or encompass.

Lucky Blighters

'They'

siphilitic: More usually spelt 'syphilitic'. An estimated 32 out of every 1,000 soldiers had syphilis by 1917. Social taboo meant that it was a disabling, though infrequently discussed, disease on the Western Front and in Britain.

Portrait of a Coward

Gloucesters: Soldiers of the Gloucestershire Regiment, with which Gurney served.

In A Soldiers' Hospital I: Pluck

dresser: Someone who dressed wounds, usually a VAD (Voluntary Aid Detachment) nurse.
clothes: Bedclothes.
woodbine: A cheap brand of untipped cigarette.

In A Soldiers' Hospital II: Gramophone Tunes

'Where did you get that girl?': A 1913 music-hall song written by Bert Kalmar and Harry Puck.

Hospital Sanctuary

chaff: Loose husks of corn left behind after harvesting.

Convalescence

cameo: A small piece of relief-carving in stone, cut in such a way as to create a light-coloured image on a darker background.
lazuli: Lapis lazuli – a blue semi-precious stone.
poppies: The red poppy (*Papaver rhoeas*) flourishes in disturbed ground and was a ubiquitous sight on the Western Front. The practice of selling artificial poppies to raise money for wounded

ex-servicemen immediately after the war resulted in it becoming an internationally recognized symbol of remembrance.

Smile, Smile, Smile

Smile, Smile, Smile: An allusion to George and Felix Powell's 'Pack Up Your Troubles', a popular song much favoured by soldiers during the First World War, which begins, 'Pack up your troubles in your old kit-bag, | And smile, smile, smile.'

Yesterday's Mail: A leading article in the *Daily Mail* for 19 September 1918 referred to society's need to provide decent and comfortable homes for soldiers returning from the war.

Vast Booty: Piratical or seafaring slang for a large amount of treasure.

The Beau Ideal

Beau Ideal: Originally the French for 'ideal beauty', a beau idéal is the perfect embodiment of a principle or quality.

Belvidere Apollos: The Apollo Belvedere, a Roman copy of a fourth-century-BC Greek statue, which has been displayed in the Pio-Clementine Museum in the Vatican since 1503 and is a byword for male beauty.

maggot: A whimsical fancy.

tittle: A tiny amount.

cicatrices: The scars or impressions left by healed wounds.

who troth with Rose would plight: Who would wish to marry Rose.

dight: Clad.

A Child's Nightmare

Morphia: Morphine, a narcotic extracted from opium, is used as a painkiller and a sedative.

Mental Cases

purgatorial: Causing mental anguish.

fretted sockets: Strained eyes.

sloughs: A slough is both a swamp and also the layer of dead tissue formed on the surface of a wound.

Rucked: Creased or wrinkled.

rope-knouts: The knots on the end of a cat-o'-nine-tails, a type of flail used up until the mid nineteenth century to punish sailors.

smote: Hit.

The Death-Bed

Aqueous: Watery.

opiate: A drug from the opium family, known for soporific and painkilling qualities. Opiates are highly addictive and, in this sense, are a drug which relieves someone of their senses.

wraiths: Things which appear suggestive of a ghost.

5 PEACE
Everyone Sang

'When this bloody war is over'

Sung to the tune of the hymn 'What a friend we have in Jesus', by Joseph M. Scriven and Charles C. Converse.

civvy: Civilian.

flue: The chimney of a stove.

Preparations for Victory

hags: Dialect for 'torments' or 'terrifies'.

jags: Sharp fragments.

Caliban: The misshapen son of the witch Sycorax in William Shakespeare's *The Tempest* (1611).

'Après la guerre finie'

Sung to the tune of 'Sous les Ponts de Paris', by Jean Rodor and Vincent Scotto.

Après la guerre finie: French for 'After the war has finished'.

Soldat anglais parti: 'The English soldier left', though it can also be read as a pun: 'The English soldier celebrated.'

Mam'selle Fransay boko pleuray: More properly, 'Mademoiselle française beaucoup pleurais' or 'The young Frenchwoman cried a lot.'

It Is Near Toussaints

Toussaints: All Saints' Day, 1 November – the feast-day in honour of all saints.

Hilaire Belloc: The essayist, poet and travel writer (1870–1953).

the night of the dead: 2 November – the feast-day for the commemoration of the souls of the dead.

Michael, Nicholas, Maries: Ancient churches in Gloucester.

the old City: Gloucester.

no bon: British soldiers' French for 'no good', this phrase was widely used on the Western Front to mean not only 'bad', but also 'broken' or 'destroyed'.

Report on Experience

Seraphina: Blunden may have in mind St Seraphina of San Gimignano (d. 1253), known for her self-denial and acts of penance as a young girl, or the Blessed Seraphina Sforza of Urbino (1434–78), whose life was one of incessant prayer, especially for the conversion of her wicked husband. However, seraphina are also female members of the highest order of angels.

Eden: 'And the Lord God planted a garden eastward in Eden; and there he put the man whom he had formed' (Genesis 2:8).

lyric: A short poem intended to be sung.

Dead and Buried

I have borne my cross: Kennedy uses various scriptural accounts
of Christ's crucifixion, death and burial throughout this poem.
Here he echoes John 19:17: 'And he bearing his cross went
forth into a place called the place of a skull, which is called
in the Hebrew Golgotha.'

I was scourged: Before his crucifixion, Jesus is severely flogged
or, as it is called in John 19:1, 'scourged'.

pierced and bleeding: In John 19:34, after Jesus has died during
his crucifixion, 'One of the soldiers with a spear pierced his
side, and forthwith came there out blood and water.'

Seine: The river that runs through Paris. The Paris Peace
Conference opened on 12 January 1919. Only Allied leaders
were allowed to attend.

brake my legs: Breaking the legs of the crucified hastened death.
According to John 19:33, 'But when they came to Jesus, and
saw that he was dead already, they brake not his legs.'

wrapped my mangled body . . . perfume: 'Then took they the
body of Jesus, and wound it in linen clothes with the spices,
as the manner of the Jews is to bury' (John 19:40).

laid it in the tomb: 'Now in the place where he was crucified
there was a garden; and in the garden a new sepulchre,
wherein was never man yet laid. There laid they Jesus' (John
19:41–2).

Versailles: The Treaty of Versailles, the peace agreement between
Germany and the Allies, was signed on 28 June 1919, and
was named after the palace in which it was signed.

made fast the open door: According to Mark 15:46, the tomb
in which Jesus was laid was sealed by rolling a stone across
the entrance.

the Council: See 'Now the chief priests, and elders, and all the council, sought false witness against Jesus, to put him to death' (Matthew 26:59). Two representatives from each of the 'Big Five' nations – France, Great Britain, Italy, Japan and the United States – met from the start as the Council of Ten to deal with immediate military and humanitarian problems. This quickly became the forum for most of the significant discussions of territorial questions, and a summit council of four, excluding Japan, was established in March 1919.

the Prince of Peace: Another name for Christ, from the prophecy in Isaiah 9:6: 'For unto us a child is born, unto us a son is given: and the government shall be upon his shoulder: and his name shall be called Wonderful, Counsellor, The mighty God, The everlasting Father, The Prince of Peace'.

The Dead and the Living

The Cenotaph

Cenotaph: The original Cenotaph (named from the Greek for 'empty tomb') was designed by Edwin Lutyens and built of wood and plaster for use on Peace Day on 19 July 1919. It was re-created in Portland marble in time for the second commemoration of the Armistice, on 11 November 1920.

huckster: A person ready to make profit from anything, however small.

The Silence

The Silence: The practice of observing two minutes' silence at 11 a.m. every 11 November commemorates the moment when hostilities ceased on the Western Front in 1918 and the Armistice came into effect. It was instigated in 1919 as a symbol of remembrance, and has since become an opportunity to remember the dead of all wars.

hoar: Grey or frosty.

down: A gently rolling hill.

The Altar of Remembrance: A poeticism for the Cenotaph.

Mecca: The spiritual centre of Islam, believed to be the birthplace of the prophet Muhammad, and the direction towards which all Muslims in the world orient their prayer mats. Every Muslim who can afford it is expected to undertake a pilgrimage to Mecca at least once in his or her life.

smite: Strike or deal a blow, often with a sword.

Armistice Day, 1921

Armistice Day: Armistice Day was first celebrated on 11 November 1919, and is now the day on which the dead of all wars are remembered with two minutes of silence.

arrested: Halted.

barrel-organs: Musical instruments in which turning a handle produces a sound. Commonly used by beggars, many of whom after the war were ex-soldiers left without employment.

'Out of the Mouths of Babes –'

'Out of the Mouths of Babes –': The title is an allusion to Psalms 8.2: 'Out of the mouth of babes and sucklings hast thou ordained strength because of thine enemies'. The phrase also appears in Matthew 21.16: 'And Jesus saith unto them, Yea; have ye never read, Out of the mouth of babes and sucklings thou hast perfected praise?'

ring the cross: Surround the war memorial, which was often in the shape of a cross.

Memorial Tablet

'In proud and glorious memory': A common phrase on many
   war memorials and gravestones.

Elegy in a Country Churchyard

Elegy in a Country Churchyard: The title alludes to the poem
   of the same name, a meditation upon the nature of death and
   fame, by Thomas Gray (1716–71).
conclave: A private meeting, especially of cardinals in the Catholic
   Church electing a new pope.

Epitaph on an Army of Mercenaries

Written after the First Battle of Ypres, in 1914, when the press
made much of the distinction between those soldiers who had
joined the army before the war and what Housman calls 'mercen-
aries' – those soldiers who had volunteered after the outbreak
of hostilities.

On Passing the New Menin Gate

Menin Gate: Designed by Sir Reginald Blomfield, the Menin Gate
   at Ypres was unveiled on 24 July 1927. Made of French lime-
   stone, it lists the 54,900 names of those who fought and died
   near Ypres and whose bodies were never found. At 8 o'clock
   each evening the local police stop traffic from passing under-
   neath the gate, and the Last Post is played. This will continue
   until the Last Post has been played for every man named on
   the memorial.
Their name liveth for ever: 'Their name liveth for evermore' is
   inscribed on all Stones of Remembrance, designed by Edwin
   Lutyens to represent those of all faiths and none, in British
   war cemeteries containing more than 1,000 graves. The quota-

tion was chosen by Rudyard Kipling from the Apocrypha: 'Their bodies are buried in peace; but their name liveth for evermore' (Ecclesiasticus 44:14).

immolation: Sacrificial slaughter of a victim, or the deliberate destruction of something for the sake of something else.

sepulchre: A tomb built from stone.

Hugh Selwyn Mauberley: V

Hugh Selwyn Mauberley: The titular hero of Pound's poem is a fictitious character loosely based on Pound himself.

Quick: Alive. See 'Who shall give account to him that is ready to judge the quick and the dead' (1 Peter 4:5).

gross: An amount equal to twelve dozen, or 144.

War and Peace

To old men's stools: To jobs as office clerks alongside those who were too old to fight in the war.

Disabled

peg: A short drink, usually of whisky.

giddy jilts: Scots slang for 'flighty women'.

daggers in plaid socks: A knife called a skean-dhu is worn in the top of a stocking as part of traditional Scottish Highland dress, and has been adopted by certain Scottish regiments.

Esprit de corps: Regimental spirit.

Strange Hells

Gloucester soldiers: Soldiers of the Gloucestershire Regiment, with which Gurney served.

diaphragms: The diaphragm is the large muscle, just below the ribcage, which controls the expansion of the lungs.

State-doles: The first Unemployment Benefit Act was passed in

1913. In 1919 it was expanded to take in all the people who had contributed to the war effort, and the benefits paid were given the unofficial name of 'the dole' because they had not been 'earned' by contributions and were therefore 'doled' out irrespective.

tatterns: Ragged, tatty clothing.

'Have you forgotten yet?'

Festubert, 1916

This poem was retitled '1916 as seen from 1921' when it was republished in *Poems 1914–30* (London: Cobden Sanderson, 1930).
breastwork: Festubert had a well-established trench called the 'Northern Breastwork'.
Shrewd: Sharply.

Lamplight

crossed swords in the Army List: A mark signifying that the soldier concerned had been wounded or killed in action – the Army List is the official register of commissioned officers serving in the British army.
A scarlet cross on my breast: A reference to the white linen aprons decorated with a red cross worn by nurses during the war.

Recalling War

silvered clean: Silver nitrate is a powerful antiseptic.
The track: Scar tissue.
a switch: A thin, flexible stick cut from a tree.

War Books

Cotswold: The Cotswolds are an area of great natural beauty in central England.

Aftermath

gagged days: The Defence of the Realm Act, passed by the House of Commons on 8 August 1914, gave the government wide-ranging powers to control daily life in Britain, including what was said and written about the war.

The Midnight Skaters

hop-poles: Poles driven into the ground upon which the plants used in brewing are grown.

Ancient History

Adam: The first man created by God: 'And the Lord God formed man of the dust of the ground, and breathed into his nostrils the breath of life; and man became a living soul' (Genesis 2:7). *Cain* and *Abel* were his sons: 'And Cain talked with Abel his brother: and it came to pass, when they were in the field, that Cain rose up against Abel his brother, and slew him' (Genesis 4:8).

The War Generation: Ave

This poem is dated 1932.
Ave: Latin for 'Hail!'

To a Conscript of 1940

Qui n'as pas . . . un héros: 'He who has not once despaired of honour will never be a hero.'
Georges Bernanos: The French Catholic novelist and essayist (1888–1948). He wrote most of his major fiction between 1926 and 1937.
fretted: Ornamented as with jewels.

Coda: Ancre Sunshine

Claire: Claire Margaret Poynting was Blunden's third wife. They were married on 29 May 1945.

lea: A tract of open ground, usually meadow, pasture or arable land.

A Glossary of the Western Front

Cross-references are indicated by *italic* type.

Aisne A département in the north-east of France, named after the river which bisects it to the south. 'Aisne' was the name given to the third phase of the German Spring Offensive that began on 27 May 1918.

Albert A town seven kilometres south-west of *Bapaume*. It was captured by the Germans in March 1918 and recaptured by the British five months later.

Allemand or **Alleyman** The French for 'German' or its equivalent in soldiers' slang.

Ancre A river that rises south of *Bapaume* and flows to the *Somme*. It gave its name to a battle fought there in November 1916.

après la guerre finie French for 'after the war has finished'. Used by soldiers and civilians alike, often sarcastically.

Arras A town on the river Scarpe, located twenty kilometres north of *Bapaume*, and the scene of heavy fighting in the autumn of 1914 and in April 1917.

Aubers Ridge Aubers Ridge was four kilometres from *Laventie* on the *Somme* battlefront.

Aveluy A small town, two kilometres north of *Albert*, and the location of the British 61st Divisional Headquarters during the war.

Bapaume A town five kilometres north-east of *Aveluy*, captured by the British in March 1917, by the Germans a year later, and finally retaken by the British in August 1918.

battalion The basic tactical infantry unit in the British army during the First World War. At full strength, it consisted of

30 officers and 977 other ranks, arranged in a battalion head-quarters and four companies.

battery An artillery unit of guns, vehicles and men.

billet A place of rest assigned to soldiers.

Blighty Soldiers' slang for 'home' or 'England', and also the name given to a wound that ensured a return to Blighty. Derived from 'bilayati', the Urdu word for 'foreign, European'.

Boche or **Bosches** Soldiers' slang for 'Germans'. Derived from French slang of uncertain origin.

bombers Soldiers armed with Mills bombs, the first safe hand-held grenade, invented by William Mills in 1915.

bolt-head See *rifle*.

breastwork See *trench*.

Cambrai A town ten kilometres east of *Bapaume* and the location of the final Allied attack on the Hindenburg Line, the system of German fortifications in the northern and central sectors of the Western Front, on 20 November 1917. German forces regained the ground they had lost by 7 December.

cartridge See *rifle*.

conscript Conscription (enforced military service) was introduced in January 1916, and was initially for unmarried men aged between eighteen and forty-one. It was extended to include married men and widowers in May 1916.

Corbie A small town fifteen kilometres east of Amiens. During the war it was used by British troops as a rest area and was the site of a casualty clearing station.

cordite An explosive, co-invented in 1889 by Sir James Dewar and Sir Frederick Abel. A blend of nitrocellulose, nitroglycerine and petroleum jelly, it gives off a strong smell but is in fact smokeless when fired.

Crucifix Corner A junction in the *trench* system on the banks of the *Ancre* near *Aveluy*, named after a dismembered crucifix that stood there.

crump See *shell*.

Dead Cow Farm This landmark lay about four kilometres due east of Neuve Eglise, a village itself about thirteen kilometres south-south-west of *Ypres*. It was so named by the British because of the presence of a number of cows' carcasses.

Death's Valley The section of the *trench* system closest to the British front *line* at Grandecourt, some six kilometres south of *Albert*, named after the biblical 'valley of the shadow of death' (Psalms 23:4).

duckboard See *trench*.

dugout See *trench*.

eighteen-pounders See *shell*.

emplacement A platform for heavy guns.

fatigues A soldier's non-combatant duties, such as digging, *wire*-mending or food preparation.

Fauquissart A small village two kilometres south-west of *Laventie*.

Festubert A small village approximately eleven kilometres south of *Laventie*.

fire-step See *trench*.

five-nines See *shell*.

Flanders The area of Belgium which was the northernmost part of the Western Front during the First World War.

flare A *cartridge* containing a signal light, fired from a special pistol – used for signalling at night or for illuminating the enemy's position. Sometimes called Very (or Verey) lights, after their inventor, Samuel W. Very.

foresight See *rifle*.

Fricourt A village about five kilometres east of *Albert*. It was one of the main objectives of the Allies on the first day of the *Somme* Offensive, but it remained in enemy hands.

Frise A village on the banks of the river *Somme*, about eight kilometres west of Peronne.

Fritz Soldiers' slang for a German or Germans. The familiar form of 'Friedrich'.

front See *line*.

fusilier A member of a British army regiment originally armed with light muskets.

gone West Soldiers' slang for 'died'.

Gonnehem A small town fifteen kilometres south-west of *Laventie*, and the scene of fierce fighting during the 1918 Spring Offensive.

High Wood Known by the French as Bois de Fourneaux (Furnace Wood), this was a prominent wooded area on the *Somme* and the scene of heavy fighting throughout the summer of 1916.

home service Military duty in one's own country. During the First World War, a significant percentage of soldiers remained on home service, carrying out transport, clerical, farming and maintenance duties.

Hun Soldiers' slang for a German. Derived from a speech given by the *Kaiser* in July 1900, when he drew a parallel between his and Attila the Hun's troops: 'Just as the Huns a thousand years ago . . . gained a reputation in virtue of which they still live in historical tradition, so may the name of Germany become known.'

Jack Johnson See *shell*.

Kaiser or **Kaiser Bill** Kaiser Wilhelm II (1859–1941) was Emperor of Germany from 1888 until 9 November 1918, when he abdicated and fled to Holland.

khaki From 'kaki', the Urdu for 'dust-coloured', and the name given to the light green-brown material used to make the uniforms of the British Expeditionary Force.

Last Post A bugle call traditionally sounded to signal the end of the military day, frequently accompanied by the order 'Lights out!'. It is also played at military funerals and services of commemoration.

Laventie A town in *Flanders*, about thirty kilometres south of *Ypres*, where troops were stationed during the war.

Lewis gun A light machine gun developed by the United States in 1911 and adopted by the British army in 1915. Although it was too heavy for efficient portable use, it became the standard support weapon for the infantry during the war.

lights out See *Last Post*.

limber The detachable front of a gun carriage.

line A military term describing the arrangement of *trench*es on the Western Front. In any given month, troops spent between three and seven days in the front-line or first-line trench, which directly faced the enemy. They would then withdraw to the support line for a similar period of time, and then go back to the reserve-line trench. After this, a week was spent 'on rest' before returning to the front line (frequently abbreviated to just 'the line'). The phrase 'the front', however, refers to the front line, support line and reserve line.

loophole See *trench*.

Loos A town approximately twenty-three kilometres north-east of *Ypres*. In the secondary phase of a major Allied offensive on the Western Front in autumn 1915, the British First Army's six divisions attacked and captured Loos on 25 September, but were thrown back on 13 October. The offensive cost the British Expeditionary Force 50,000 casualties.

Lord Derby's scheme A voluntary recruitment scheme instigated by the Director of Recruiting, Lord Derby (1865–1948), in July 1915. 'Derby Men' enlisted in the army and served for just one day, before returning to their civilian occupations to await being called up according to age and occupation.

lyddite See *shell*.

Mametz Wood Four kilometres north-east of *Albert* and the scene of heavy fighting during the early days of the *Somme* Offensive in July 1916.

Menin Road The main road leading east from *Ypres* and the scene of some of the heaviest fighting by the British Expeditionary Force on the Western Front, particularly during the First and Third Battles of Ypres.

mess-tins Square metal tins used by soldiers for washing and eating.

Miraumont A village two kilometres north-east of Grandcourt, which remained in German hands during the *Somme* Offensive, being captured by the British only in February 1917. The village is split into two sections by the river *Ancre*.

Mons A city approximately sixty-five kilometres south-west of Brussels and close to the border of France. Mons was the site of the first major engagement for the British Expeditionary Force in August and September 1914, as well as the site of the closing battles of the war.

mustard gas A heavy yellow poisonous gas and blistering agent, dichlorodiethylsulphide, first used by the Germans against the Russians at Riga in September 1917. Its effects on the eyes, throat and lungs were devastating, and it possessed an unfortunate tendency to remain in *shell* holes and then be dispersed by later shelling.

NCO Non-commissioned officer – anyone above the rank of *private*, and below the rank of second lieutenant in the British army.

no man's land The space between opposing *trenches*, so called because it belonged to 'no man'.

Old Contemptibles The survivors of the regular army who fought in the earliest battles of the war, before the introduction of volunteers or *conscripts*. So called because of the *Kaiser*'s alleged comment that he was being opposed by a 'contemptible little army'.

Ovillers A village on the *Somme* battlefront approximately four

kilometres north-east of *Albert*, used mainly for soldiers'
billets.

parados See *trench*.

parapet See *trench*.

Passchendaele A wood and village eleven kilometres east-north-
east of *Ypres*. The ridge at Passchendaele was the last objec-
tive taken in the Third Battle of Ypres, and has since been
used as a synonym for this battle.

phosgene Carbonyl chloride, an extremely poisonous and colour-
less gas, first used by the Germans on 31 May 1915 against
Russian troops in Bzura and Rawka in Poland. Only a small
amount was needed to render a soldier ineffective, and it
killed its victims within forty-eight hours.

Picardie/Picard/Picardy An area of France that includes the *Aisne*,
Oise and *Somme* regions, and the scene of the majority of
the fighting by the British Expeditionary Force during the war.

private The lowest rank in the British army.

redoubt A temporary fortification, typically square or polygonal
in shape, without flanking defences.

respirator A gas mask.

rifle The bolt-head is the sliding piece of the breech mechanism
of a rifle, into which a cartridge – a metal case containing
propellant explosive and a bullet – is placed. The foresight is
the front sight of the rifle, through which the user must look
in order to pinpoint his target accurately. The rifle-thong is
the strap attached to the rifle, used to carry it over the shoul-
der. The stock is the butt of the rifle.

rum ration A tradition adopted from the navy, whereby soldiers
were issued with a daily quantity of rum.

Saint-Eloi A town in *Flanders*, four kilometres south of *Ypres*
on the Ypres–Messines Road.

salient An area where the *line* bulges out towards the enemy and
therefore often has to be defended from three sides at once.

The most famous salient surrounded the town of *Ypres* in Belgium, which was destroyed during the war.

sap See *trench*.

Senlis A village on the river Nonette, a tributary of the Oise, fifty-one kilometres north of Paris and ten kilometres east of Chantilly, frequented by troops on rest.

shell An explosive projectile, fired from a large gun and often containing the high explosive lyddite. Shells were often known by their size or weight, as in the case of 'five-nines', 'twelve-inch', 'six-inch' and 'eighteen-pounders', or were given nicknames such as 'whizz-bang' or 'crump' because of the noise they made. 'Jack Johnsons' were named after the African-American boxer Jack Johnson (1878–1946), because of their power and the black smoke they made on detonation.

shell shock First diagnosed in 1914, shell shock was the generic name given to the psychological disturbance caused by prolonged exposure to active warfare. Frequently expressed through physical symptoms such as muteness and paralysis of the limbs, it was so called because it was believed to be caused by exposure to the vacuum created by *shells* exploding nearby.

shot A coarse, non-explosive lead bullet.

shrapnel *Shell* fragments thrown out by an explosion.

six-inch See *shell*.

Somme The river Somme flows through northern France to the English Channel and is 240 kilometres long. Concentrated on the eastern part of the river, the Somme Offensive took place between 1 July and 18 November 1916 and is remembered for the 60,000 British casualties sustained on the first day, of which 20,000 were fatalities. The battle was the largest and most sustained offensive by the British Expeditionary Force during the war.

stock See *rifle*.

tank Tanks were first used during the latter stages of the *Somme* Offensive, at Delville Wood on 15 September 1916. Also called 'landships', they were supplied by the British navy and were given the code name 'tank' because of their resemblance to water carriers.

Tommy The traditional nickname of the British soldier, derived from 'Thomas Atkins', the name used in specimen official forms in the nineteenth century.

traversing Firing a rifle or shelling horizontally in a sweeping motion.

trench A model trench was just under two metres deep, with duckboards of narrow slatted wood covering the ground. The sides of the trench were known as breastworks, the side facing the enemy being the parapet and the rear side being the parados. The parapet had a raised fire-step on which a soldier stood to fire his weapon. The trench was protected by barbed wire and by walls of sandbags containing loopholes, narrow slits through which soldiers could fire or look. Saps were narrower trenches which extended into *no man's land* and were used primarily for communication. A dugout was a roofed shelter dug into the sides of the trench, and was also known ironically as a 'funk-hole'.

twelve-inch See *shell*.

Vlamertinghe A village five kilometres west of *Ypres* which suffered many heavy bombardments throughout the war.

whizz-bangs See *shell*.

wire Work in the *trenches* often consisted of repairing or laying barbed wire in *no man's land*, usually at night.

Ypres A Belgian town on the Western Front, heavily contested by both sides and eventually destroyed as a result. The three battles of Ypres took place between 31 October and 17

November 1914, 22 April and 25 May 1915, and 31 July and 10 November 1917. Known as 'Wipers' in soldiers' slang.

Biographies

[Arthur] St John Adcock was born in London in 1864. After working as a lawyer, he became a full-time writer in 1893. He was made acting editor of *The Bookman* in 1908, and succeeded to the editorship in 1923. He died in 1930.

'The Silence' first appeared in *Collected Poems of St. John Adcock* (London: Hodder & Stoughton, 1929).

Richard Aldington was born in Portsmouth, Hampshire, in 1882 and was educated at Dover College and at University College, London. He volunteered in 1914, but was rejected on medical grounds. He successfully enlisted in May 1916 and served in France from November 1916, initially in the ranks of the 11th Devonshire Regiment before becoming an NCO in the 6th Leicestershire Regiment. He was commissioned as a second lieutenant in the 3rd Royal Sussex Regiment in November 1917, only to be severely gassed and shell-shocked in the following year. One of the founders of the Imagist Movement in poetry, he had a successful post-war career as a poet, novelist and biographer, and *Death of a Hero* (London: Chatto & Windus, 1929) and *Roads to Glory* (London: Chatto & Windus, 1930) are fictionalized accounts of his war experiences. He died in 1962.

'Bombardment', 'In the Trenches' and 'Soliloquy II' were first published in *Images of War* (London: George Allen & Unwin, 1919). 'Reserve' appeared in *Images of Desire* (London: Elkin Matthews, 1919).

Martin Armstrong was born in Newcastle upon Tyne in 1882 and was educated at Charterhouse and at Pembroke College,

Cambridge. A writer before the war, he enlisted as a private in the 28th (County of London) Battalion of the London Regiment (The Artists' Rifles), was commissioned in the following year in the Middlesex Regiment, and went on to serve on the Western Front. After the war he worked as a literary journalist, short-story writer, novelist and anthologist. He died in 1974.

'Before the Battle' appeared in *The Bird-Catcher and Other Poems* (London: Martin Secker, 1929).

Herbert Asquith was born in London in 1881 and was educated at Winchester College and at Balliol College, Oxford. The son of Herbert Henry Asquith, Prime Minister between 1908 and 1916, he was called to the Bar in 1907. Receiving a commission in the Royal Marine Artillery at the end of 1914, he served as a second lieutenant with an anti-aircraft battery in France before being wounded in June 1915 and sent home. In June 1916 he joined the Royal Field Artillery and returned to France, ending the war with the rank of captain. He died in 1947.

'The Volunteer' appeared in *The Volunteer and Other Poems* (London: Sidgwick & Jackson, 1915).

Maurice Baring was born in London in 1874, the fourth son of Lord Revelstoke, and was educated at Eton and at Trinity College, Cambridge. He joined the diplomatic service and then became a foreign correspondent for *The Times* and the *Morning Post*. During the war he worked in military intelligence as a secretary and interpreter and was attached to the Royal Flying Corps headquarters in both France and England. At the close of the war he had achieved the rank of major, and he was awarded an OBE for his wartime services. He had a successful post-war career as a novelist, dramatist, translator and critic. His *R.F.C. H.Q., 1914–1918* (London: G. Bell & Sons, 1920) is an account of his wartime experiences. He died in 1945.

'August, 1918' appeared in *Poems: 1914–1919* (London: Martin Secker, 1920).

Pauline Barrington was born in Philadelphia in 1876 and worked for most of her life as a secretary, while at the same time contributing poetry, short stories and reviews to various magazines. The date of her death is unknown.

'Education' appeared in *Poems Written During the Great War 1914–1918: An Anthology*, ed. Bertram Lloyd (London: George Allen & Unwin, 1918).

Laurence Binyon was born in Lancaster in 1869 and was educated at St Paul's School and at Trinity College, Oxford, where he won the Newdigate Prize for poetry. He worked in the British Museum's Department of Printed Books until 1916, when he went to the Western Front as a Red Cross orderly. After the war he returned to the British Museum, and in 1932 he became keeper of the Department of Prints and Drawings. He was a prolific author, publishing widely on oriental art and producing many collections of poetry. He died in 1943.

'For the Fallen' appeared in *The Winnowing-Fan: Poems on the Great War* (London: Elkin Matthews, 1914). 'The Sower' appeared in *The New World* (London: Elkin Matthews, 1918).

Edmund Blunden was born in London in 1896 and grew up in Yalding in Kent. Educated at Christ's Hospital and at Queen's College, Oxford, he joined the 11th Battalion of the Royal Sussex Regiment (1st South Downs) as a second lieutenant on the outbreak of the First World War. He fought on the Somme and at Ypres, winning the Military Cross and eventually being promoted to full lieutenant. After the war he held several academic posts, including professorships of English Literature at Tokyo University, at the University of Hong Kong and at Oxford

University, and he won the Queen's Gold Medal for Poetry in 1956. His war experiences are recounted in *Undertones of War* (London: Cobden-Sanderson, 1928). He died in 1974.

'Festubert, 1916' appeared in *The Shepherd and Other Poems* (London: Cobden-Sanderson, 1922). 'Illusions' and 'Vlamertinghe: Passing the Chateau, July, 1917' appeared in *Undertones of War* (London: Cobden-Sanderson, 1928). 'At Senlis Once', 'Preparations for Victory' and 'The Midnight Skaters' appeared in *Masks of Time: A New Collection of Poems Principally Meditative* (London: Beaumont Press, 1925). 'Report on Experience' appeared in *Near and Far: New Poems* (London: Cobden-Sanderson, 1929). 'Ancre Sunshine' appeared in *Overtones of War: Poems of the First World War*, ed. Martin Taylor (London: Duckworth, 1996).

Vera Brittain was born in Newcastle under Lyme in 1896, but spent her childhood in Macclesfield and Buxton. Educated at St Monica's, Kingswood, and at Somerville College, Oxford, she had her studies interrupted by the outbreak of war, and in 1915 she joined the Voluntary Aid Detachment as a nurse and served in London, Malta and France. She was one of the first women to graduate from Oxford after the war, and throughout her life she was heavily involved in socialism and the feminist movement. Her wartime experiences are recounted in *Testament of Youth* (London: Victor Gollancz, 1933) and in her diary *Chronicle of Youth* (London: Victor Gollancz, 1981). She died in 1970.

'Hospital Sanctuary', 'The Superfluous Woman' and 'The War Generation: *Ave*' appeared in *Poems of the War and After* (London: Victor Gollancz, 1934).

Rupert Brooke was born in Rugby in 1887, the son of a housemaster at Rugby School. He was educated there and at King's College, Cambridge. His first book of verse, *Poems* (London:

Sidgwick & Jackson), appeared in 1911. Two years later he became a fellow of King's and then embarked upon a year-long journey around America and the South Seas. Enlisting in the Anson Battalion of the Royal Naval Reserve when war broke out, he saw action in Antwerp in October 1914. Transferring to the Hood Battalion for the Gallipoli Offensive, he contracted septicaemia from a mosquito bite and died on the Greek island of Skyros on St George's Day, 1915.

'1914: Peace', '1914: Safety', '1914: The Dead' (both poems) and '1914: The Soldier' appeared in *1914 and Other Poems* (London: Sidgwick & Jackson, 1915). 'Fragment' appeared in *The Collected Poems of Rupert Brooke: With a Memoir* (London: Sidgwick & Jackson, 1918).

May Wedderburn Cannan was born in Oxford in 1893 and was educated at Wychwood School. She joined the Voluntary Aid Detachment in 1911, training as a nurse and eventually reaching the rank of quartermaster. During the war she spent four weeks in France, working as an auxiliary nurse at Rouen, before returning to England, where she joined the Oxford University Press and became involved in publishing material produced by the government's War Propaganda Bureau. She also worked for Military Intelligence in Paris for a short period. Her autobiography, *Grey Ghosts and Voices* (Kineton: Roundwood Press, 1976), did not appear until after her death in 1973.

'Lamplight' appeared in *In War Time* (Oxford: B. H. Blackwell, 1917). 'Paris, November 11, 1918' appeared in *The Splendid Days* (Oxford: B. H. Blackwell, 1919).

G[ilbert] K[eith] Chesterton was born in London in 1874. He was educated at St Paul's School, going on to study simultaneously at the Slade School of Art and University College, London. He drifted into journalism, which he later claimed was his sole profession, but he also wrote novels, poetry, and religious and political essays. A Catholic apologist, he is probably best known for his popular Father Brown detective stories. He died in 1936.

'Elegy in a Country Churchyard' appeared in *The Ballad of St. Barbara and Other Verses* (London: Cecil Palmer, 1922).

Margaret Postgate Cole was born in Cambridge in 1893 and was educated at Roedean and at Girton College, Cambridge. She taught Classics at St Paul's Girls School in London for a short time, before taking up political work in the Fabian Research Department in 1917. In 1918 she moved to Oxford, where she taught evening classes and worked part-time for the Labour Research Department. In later life, when she was a Labour Party member of the London County Council, Cole was an important figure in the early experiments with comprehensive education. She wrote many books during her lifetime, including political works and detective novels. She was made an OBE in 1965 and a Dame of the British Empire in 1970. She died in 1980.

'The Veteran' appeared in *An Anthology of War Poems*, ed. Frederick Brereton (London: W. Collins Sons & Co., 1930).

Lesley Coulson was born in 1889 in Kilburn, London. Well known as a journalist before the war, he rose to become assistant editor of the *Morning Post*. In August 1914 he enlisted as a private in the 2nd Battalion of the London Regiment (Royal Fusiliers). He was wounded at Gallipoli in 1915. Preferring not to seek a commission, he was promoted to sergeant and sent to France. Now attached to the 12th Battalion of the London Regiment (The Rangers), he was killed during a British attack on the German stronghold position of Dewdrop Trench on 8 October 1916.

'War' appeared in *From an Outpost, and Other Poems* (London: Erskine Macdonald, 1917).

Nancy Cunard was born at Nevill Holt, Leicestershire, in 1896, the daughter of Sir Bache and Lady Cunard, and was educated privately in London, Germany and Paris. She settled in Paris during the 1920s and became involved in bohemian society, posing as a model for Oskar Kokoschka and Percy Wyndham Lewis. During the Spanish Civil War (1936–9), she went to Spain as a correspondent for the *Manchester Guardian*, and she worked for the Free French in London during the Second World War. She died in 1965.

'Zeppelins' appeared in *Outlaws* (London: Elkin Matthews, 1921).

Walter de la Mare was born in Charlton, Kent, in 1873 and was educated at St Paul's Cathedral School. At the age of sixteen he left St Paul's to take up a career in accountancy with the Anglo-American Oil Company. Awarded a government pension of £100 per year for his imaginative writing in 1908, he took up writing full-time. He was made a Companion of Honour in 1948, and in 1953 was made a member of the Order of Merit. He died in 1956.

'The Marionettes' appeared in *Motley and Other Poems* (London: Constable & Co., 1918).

Eva Dobell was born in Cheltenham in 1867. She spent most of her life in the Cotswolds, but travelled extensively in Europe and Africa. She worked as a nurse during the war, and was a children's author and an active conservationist throughout her life. She died in 1973.

'In A Soldiers' Hospital I: Pluck' and 'In A Soldiers' Hospital II: Gramophone Tunes' appeared in *A Bunch of Cotswold Grasses* (London: Arthur H. Stockwell, 1919).

Helen Parry Eden was born in London in 1885 and was educated at Roedean, at Manchester University and at King's College Art

School. A prolific poet, she contributed verse to *Punch*, the *Pall Mall Magazine* and other journals. The date of her death is unknown.

'The Admonition: To Betsey' appeared in *Coal and Candlelight and Other Verses* (London: John Lane, 1918).

Geoffrey Faber was born in Malvern in 1889 and was educated at Rugby and at both Christ Church and All Souls, Oxford. Commissioned as a second lieutenant in the 3rd Glamorgan Battery of the Royal Field Artillery in November 1914, he transferred to the 2/8th Battalion of the City of London Regiment (The Post Office Rifles) in February 1915. After promotion to temporary lieutenant in September, he became a captain in March 1916 and served in France between January 1917 and January 1919. A publisher by profession, he was the founder and first president of Faber & Faber. He was knighted in 1954, and he died in 1961.

'The Eve of War' appeared in *Interflow: Poems Chiefly Lyrical* (London: Constable & Co., 1915). 'Home Service' appeared in *The Buried Stream: Collected Poems 1908 to 1940* (London: Faber & Faber, 1941).

Eleanor Farjeon was born in London in 1881 and was educated privately. During the war she contributed regularly to *Punch*, and between 1917 and 1930 she wrote verse (as 'Tomfool') for the *Daily Herald*. A staff member of *Time and Tide* in the 1920s, she is best known today for her children's verse and short stories and as author of the words of the popular hymn 'Morning Has Broken'. She won the Library Association Carnegie Medal in 1956. She died in 1965.

'Now that you too must shortly go the way' appeared in *Sonnets and Poems* (Oxford: Basil Blackwell, 1918). 'Easter Monday' appeared in *First and Second Love* (London: Michael Joseph, 1947).

Gilbert Frankau was born in London in 1884 and was educated at Eton. He worked in the family tobacco business, and spent two years travelling around the world between 1912 and 1914. He was commissioned as a second lieutenant in the 9th East Surrey Regiment ('The Gallants') in October 1914, and transferred to the 107th Brigade of the Royal Field Artillery in March 1915. He served at Loos, Ypres and the Somme, and in Italy, but was invalided out of the army with the rank of captain in February 1918. He was a popular and prolific inter-war novelist and a squadron leader in the RAF during the Second World War. His war experiences are fictionalized in *Peter Jackson, Cigar Merchant* (London: Hutchinson & Co., 1920). He died in 1954.

'Headquarters' appeared in *The Guns* (London: Chatto & Windus, 1916). 'The Deserter' and 'Wife and Country' appeared in *The Judgement of Valhalla* (London: Chatto & Windus, 1918).

John Freeman was born in Dalston, Middlesex, in 1880, the son of a commercial traveller. Educated locally in Hackney, he left school at thirteen to work as a junior clerk at the Liverpool Victoria Friendly Society, eventually rising to become a director of the same firm. He was later appointed chief executive officer in the Department of National Health and Insurance. He was awarded the Hawthornden Prize for imaginative writing in 1924, and he died five years later, in 1929.

'Happy is England Now' appeared in *Stone Trees and Other Poems* (London: Selwyn & Blount, 1916).

Robert Frost was born in San Francisco in 1874 and moved to New England at the age of nineteen. He spent a year at both Dartford College and Harvard University, but left to teach, farm, and write poetry. From 1912 until 1915 he lived in England, where he became a friend of Edward Thomas (q.v.); upon his return to New England he devoted himself to poetry, supporting himself by teaching appointments at Amherst College and the University of Michigan. He won the Pulitzer Prize for his poetry in 1924, 1931, 1937 and 1943. He died in 1963.

'Not to Keep' appeared in *New Hampshire: A Poem with Notes and Grace Notes* (London: Grant Richards, 1924).

Wilfrid Gibson was born in Hexham, Northumberland, in 1878 and was educated locally. A published poet while still in his teens, he was a friend of Rupert Brooke (q.v.) and, with him, one of the founders of the Georgian Movement in poetry. He volunteered in 1915, but was rejected four times because of his poor eyesight. Finally accepted by the Army Service Corps, he served first as a 'loader and packer' and later as a medical officer's clerk in Sydenham. He died in 1962.

'Breakfast', 'His Mate' and 'The Question' appeared in *Battle* (London: Elkin Matthews, 1915). 'Air-Raid', 'Ragtime' and 'The Conscript' appeared in *Neighbours* (London: Macmillan & Co., 1920).

Robert Graves was born in Southwark, London, in 1895 and was educated at Charterhouse. Shortly after he left school the war broke out, and he immediately enlisted as a second lieutenant in the 3rd Battalion of the Royal Welsh Fusiliers. He saw active service on the Western Front until February 1917, when ill health resulted in his being posted for home duties in Great Britain and Ireland until his demobilization in February 1919. After a brief and unsuccessful period at St John's College, Oxford, he took up the post of Professor of English Literature at Cairo University, later moving to Majorca. He was Professor of Poetry at Oxford between 1961 and 1966. His wartime experiences are recorded in *Goodbye to All That* (London: Jonathan Cape, 1929) and *But It Still Goes On* (London: Jonathan Cape, 1930). He died in 1985.

'It's a Queer Time' appeared in *Over the Brazier* (London: Poetry

Bookshop, 1916). 'A Child's Nightmare', 'A Dead Boche', 'Dead Cow Farm', 'The Last Post' and 'Two Fusiliers' appeared in *Fairies and Fusiliers* (London: William Heinemann, 1917). 'Recalling War' appeared in *Collected Poems* (London: Cassell & Co., 1938). 'The Survivor Comes Home' appeared in *Complete Poems: Vol. 3*, ed. Beryl Graves and Dunstan Ward (Manchester: Carcanet, 1999).

Julian Grenfell was born in London in 1888, the son of Lord Desborough, and was educated at Eton and at Balliol College, Oxford. He joined the First Royal Dragoons (The Royals) in 1910 and served as a cavalry officer in India and South Africa during the next four years. On the outbreak of the First World War he was sent to France, where he was twice mentioned in dispatches and was awarded the Distinguished Service Order. He was badly wounded by shrapnel during action near Ypres, and died in hospital in Boulogne on 30 April 1915.

'Into Battle' appeared in *A Crown of Amaranth: Being a Collection of Poems to the Memory of the Brave and Gallant Gentlemen Who Gave Their Lives for Great and Greater Britain* (London: Erskine Macdonald, 1915).

Ivor Gurney was born in Gloucester in 1890, the son of a tailor. He was educated at King's School, Gloucester, and at the Royal College of Music in London, where a nervous breakdown did not prevent him from producing some of his finest song settings. He joined the 2/5th Battalion of the Gloucester Regiment in February 1915 and saw active service on the Western Front between June 1916 and September 1917. He was invalided home after being gassed during the Passchendaele Offensive, and suffered a severe mental breakdown shortly afterwards. He returned to the Royal College of Music in 1919, but his mental condition worsened again and in September 1922 he was diagnosed as a paranoid schizophrenic and was committed first to an asylum in Gloucester and then to the City of London Mental Hospital in Dartford. He died there of tuberculosis on 26 December 1937.

'Ballad of the Three Spectres' and 'Sonnets 1917: Servitude' appeared in *Severn and Somme* (London: Sidgwick & Jackson, 1917). 'To his Love' appeared in *War's Embers and Other Verses* (London: Sidgwick & Jackson, 1919). 'The Silent One', 'Strange Hells' and 'War Books' appeared in *Poems by Ivor Gurney: Principally Selected from Unpublished Manuscripts, with a Memoir by Edmund Blunden* (London: Hutchinson & Co, 1954). 'After War', 'Canadians', 'Crucifix Corner' and 'Serenade' appeared in *Poems of Ivor Gurney 1890–1937: With an Introduction by Edmund Blunden and a Bibliographical Note by Leonard Clark* (London: Chatto & Windus, 1973). 'Blighty', 'Butchers and Tombs', 'First Time In', 'It Is Near Toussaints' and 'On Somme' appeared in *Collected Poems of Ivor Gurney*, ed. P. J. Kavanagh (Oxford: Oxford University Press, 1982). 'Portrait of a Coward' appeared in *Best Poems and The Book of Five Makings*, ed. R. K. R. Thornton and George Walter (Ashington and Manchester: MidNAG and Carcanet, 1995).

Thomas Hardy was born at Upper Bockhampton in Dorset in 1840. He went to school in Dorchester, receiving private tuition in Latin and French, and practised as an architect before finding worldwide fame as a novelist, but the negative reaction to his *Jude the Obscure* (1898) led him to abandon prose for poetry. He was awarded the Order of Merit in 1910, and he died in 1928.

'Channel Firing' and 'Men Who March Away' appeared in *Satires of Circumstance: Lyrics and Reveries with Miscellaneous Pieces* (London: Macmillan & Co., 1914). 'I looked up from my writing' appeared in *Moments of Vision and Miscellaneous Verses* (London: Macmillan & Co., 1917).

F[rederick] W[illiam] Harvey was born in Hartpury, Gloucestershire, in 1888. He was educated at Rossall School, and later trained as a solicitor. Enlisting in the 1/5th Battalion of the Gloucestershire Regiment at the outbreak of war, he arrived in France in March 1915, and soon afterwards won the Distinguished Conduct Medal. He was commissioned as a second lieutenant, but was captured by the Germans in August 1916 and spent the rest of the war in camps at Crefeld and Gutersslöh. After the war he returned to practising as a solicitor, while continuing to write poetry. His war experiences are recounted in *Comrades in Captivity* (London: Sidgwick & Jackson, 1920). He died in 1957.

'If We Return' appeared in *A Gloucestershire Lad at Home and Abroad* (London: Sidgwick & Jackson, 1916). 'Prisoners' appeared in *Gloucestershire Friends: Poems from a German Prison Camp* (London: Sidgwick and Jackson, 1917). 'Out of the Mouths of Babes –' appeared in *September and Other Poems* (London: Sidgwick & Jackson, 1925).

May Herschel-Clarke. Nothing is known of this author, but 'The Mother' appeared in *Behind the Firing Line and Other Poems of the War* (London: Erskine Macdonald, 1917).

W[illiam] N[oel] Hodgson was born in Petersfield, Hampshire, in 1893 and was educated at Durham School and at Christ Church, Oxford. He was commissioned as a second lieutenant in the 9th Battalion of the Devonshire Regiment in September 1914. He was sent to France in July 1915 and was promoted to lieutenant in September, winning the Military Cross a month later. He died on the first day of the Somme Offensive, on 1 July 1916.

'Back to Rest' and 'Before Action' appeared in *Verse and Prose in Peace and War* (London: Smith, Elder & Co., 1916).

Teresa Hooley was born at Risley Lodge, Derbyshire, in 1888 and was educated by a private governess and then at Howard College, Bedford. She wrote poetry throughout her life. She died in 1973.

'A War Film' appeared in *Songs of All Seasons* (London: Jonathan Cape, 1927).

A[lfred] E[dward] Housman was born in Bromsgrove, Worcestershire, in 1859 and was educated at Bromsgrove School and at St John's College, Oxford. He worked for many years as a Higher Division Clerk in the Patent Office in London, but when the Professor of Greek and Latin at University College London died he was offered the chair on the strength of seventeen testimonials and took the seat in 1892. He went on to become a distinguished classical scholar, a poet, and, in 1911, Professor of Latin at Cambridge University. He died in 1936.

'On the idle hill of summer' appeared in *A Shropshire Lad* (London: Grant Richards, 1896). 'Epitaph on an Army of Mercenaries' appeared in *Last Poems* (London: Grant Richards, 1922).

Philip Johnstone. 'High Wood' was first published in *The Nation* on 16 February 1918, but nothing is known about its author. Frequently anthologized today, this version is taken from what seems to be its first appearance in book form in *Vain Glory: A Miscellany of the Great War 1914–1918 Written by Those Who Fought in it on Each Side and All Fronts*, ed. with an introduction by Guy Chapman (London: Cassell & Co., 1937).

G[eoffrey] A[nketell] Studdert Kennedy was born in Leeds in 1883 and was educated at Leeds Grammar School and at Trinity College, Dublin. He was ordained as an Anglican minister in

1908, and joined the Army Chaplains Department in December 1915. He had three spells in the trenches – on the Somme in 1916, at Messines Ridge in 1917, and during the final advance in 1918 – but otherwise was posted behind the lines, where he preached powerful, unconventional sermons to large congregations. He was awarded the Military Cross in 1917, and after the Armistice he continued to write poetry and to champion the underprivileged. He died in 1929.

'Dead and Buried' and 'If ye Forget' appeared in *Peace Rhymes of a Padre* (London: Hodder & Stoughton, 1920). 'Woodbine Willie' appeared in *The Sorrows of God and Other Poems* (London: Hodder & Stoughton, 1921).

Rudyard Kipling was born in Bombay in 1865 and was educated at the United Services College at Westward Ho!, Devon. He was a journalist in India between 1882 and 1889, and later became one of Britain's best-known novelists and poets. He was awarded the Nobel Prize for literature in 1907, but refused the Poet Laureateship on three occasions. He was one of the instigators of the burial of the Unknown Warrior in Westminster Abbey on 11 November 1920, and proposed the standard inscription used in British war cemeteries across the world: 'their name liveth for evermore'. He died in 1936.

'Epitaphs: A Son', 'Epitaphs: Common Form', 'Epitaphs: The Coward', 'For All We Have and Are', 'Gethsemane' and 'My Boy Jack' appeared in *The Years Between* (London: Methuen & Co., 1919).

D[avid] H[erbert] Lawrence was born in Nottingham in 1885, the son of a miner, and was educated at University College, Nottingham. A schoolteacher before turning to writing as a profession, he was a prolific novelist and short-story writer. Apart from the years spent in England during the First World War, he lived mostly abroad – in Italy, Australia and New Mexico. He died in Vence, near Nice, in 1930.

'Bombardment', 'Going Back' and 'Rondeau of a Conscientious Objector' appeared in *Bay: A Book of Poems* (London: Beaumont Press, 1919).

Amy Lowell was born into an illustrious New England family in Brookline, Massachusetts, in 1874, and was educated privately. A central figure in the Imagist Movement in poetry, she edited several anthologies of her fellow Imagists' work and became so active in the movement that Ezra Pound (q.v.) renamed it 'Amy-gism'. Her book of poetry *What's O'Clock* (Boston: Houghton Mifflin Co., 1925) was published posthumously shortly after her death in 1925 and went on to win the Pulitzer Prize.

'Convalescence' appeared in *Sword Blades and Poppy Seed* (London: Macmillan & Co., 1914).

W[alter] S[cott] S[tuart] Lyon was born in North Berwick in 1886 and was educated at Haileybury and at Balliol College, Oxford. From December 1912 he served as a territorial in the 9th Battalion (Highlanders) of the Royal Scots Regiment with the rank of lieutenant. Like all territorials, he was mobilized in August 1914, and he went to France in February of the following year. He was killed in action on 8 May 1915 during the Second Battle of Ypres.

'I tracked a dead man down a trench' appeared in *Easter at Ypres 1915 and Other Poems* (Glasgow: James Maclehose & Sons, 1916).

Rose Macaulay was born in Cambridge in 1881 but spent most of her childhood in Italy. She was educated at Somerville College, Oxford, and became a novelist, essayist, and poet, contributing regularly to *Time and Tide* and *The Spectator*. She was named a Dame of the British Empire in 1958, and died the same year.

'Picnic' appeared in *Three Days* (London: Constable & Co., 1919).

John McCrae was born in Guelph, Ontario, in 1872, and trained as a doctor at McGill University, Montreal. He served as a gunner and an officer in an artillery battery with the Canadian Contingent in the second Anglo-Boer War (1899–1902), and when the First World War broke out he joined the Canadian Army Medical Corps, sailing immediately for France as surgeon to the First Brigade of Canadian Artillery. After manning a dressing station during the Second Battle of Ypres, he was put in charge of the No. 3 General Hospital in Boulogne. In January 1918 he was appointed consultant to all the British armies in France, but he died of pneumonia before he could take up the position.

'In Flanders Fields' appeared in *In Flanders Fields and Other Poems* (London: Hodder & Stoughton Ltd, 1919).

Patrick MacGill was born near Glenties in Donegal in 1890 and was educated locally. In his own words, he worked as a 'farm servant, byer-man, drainer, potato-digger, surface-man and navvy' before joining the editorial staff of the *Daily Express* in 1911. He enlisted at the outbreak of war, and became a sergeant in the 18th London Regiment (London Irish Rifles). He went to France in March 1915, and was wounded at Loos in October that year. He published many books during his lifetime, including poetry, novels and plays. His war experiences are recounted in *The Amateur Army* (London: Herbert Jenkins, 1915), *The Red Horizon* (London: Herbert Jenkins, 1916) and *The Great Push* (London: Herbert Jenkins, 1916). He died in 1963.

'Before the Charge' appeared in *Soldier Songs* (London: Herbert Jenkins, 1917).

E[wart] A[lan] Mackintosh was born in Brighton in 1893 and was educated at St Paul's School and at Christ Church, Oxford. He left Oxford to join the 5th Battalion of the Seaforth Highlanders (The Sutherland and Caithness Highland), and in July 1915 was sent to France, where he was awarded the Military Cross in the following May. He was gassed and wounded at High Wood during the Somme Offensive and returned to England, where he trained the Cadet Corps at Cambridge. He returned to the front in 1917, and was killed at Cambrai on 21 November.

'In Memoriam Private D. Sutherland . . .' appeared in *A Highland Regiment* (London: John Lane, 1917). 'Recruiting' appeared in *War, the Liberator and Other Pieces: With a Memoir* (London: John Lane, 1918).

Frederic Manning was born in Sydney, Australia, in 1882, and was educated privately. To complete his studies, he was sent to England, where he established a reputation as a minor poet and critic. He enlisted as a private in the 7th Battalion of the King's Shropshire Light Infantry in 1915, and served in France for the next two years. He was commissioned as a second lieutenant in the 3rd Battalion of the Royal Irish Regiment in May 1917, but his poor health prevented further active service and he was demobilized in March 1918. His war experiences are recounted in fictional form in *The Middle Parts of Fortune* (London: Piazza Press, 1929), reissued a year later in an expurgated edition as *Her Privates We* (London: Peter Davies, 1930). He died in 1935.

'Grotesque' and 'The Face' appeared in *Eidola* (London: John Murray, 1917).

John Masefield was born in Ledbury, Herefordshire, in 1878 and was educated at King's School, Warwick, and on board the training ship HMS *Conway*. Between 1895 and 1897 he lived in New York, working as a bartender and in a carpet factory. On his return to England he worked as a journalist, poet and playwright, finding fame with *The Everlasting Mercy* (London: Sidgwick & Jackson, 1911), a narrative poem deemed shocking at the time because of its realism. On the outbreak of war he became an orderly at a British Red Cross hospital in France, and in 1915 he took charge of a motor-boat ambulance service at Gallipoli. He was appointed Poet Laureate in 1930, and was awarded the Order of Merit in 1935. He died in 1967.

'August, 1914' appeared in *Philip the King and Other Poems* (London: William Heinemann, 1914).

Charlotte Mew was born in Bloomsbury, London, in 1869 and was educated at the Lucy Harrison School for Girls in Gower Street. Throughout her life she was beset with ill health, family deaths and poverty, but the award of a Civil List Pension of £75 per annum in 1923, on the recommendation of Thomas Hardy, John Masefield and Walter de la Mare (qq.v.), allowed her to write. In 1928 she committed suicide by drinking disinfectant while undergoing treatment for her neurasthenia.

'The Cenotaph' appeared in *The Farmer's Bride* (2nd edn: London: Poetry Bookshop, 1921). 'May, 1915' appeared in *The Rambling Sailor* (London: Poetry Bookshop, 1929).

Harold Monro was born in Brussels, Belgium, in 1879 and was educated at Radley College and at Caius College, Cambridge. He founded the *Poetry Review* in 1912, was the publisher of the Georgian Poetry series, and opened and ran the Poetry Bookshop in London from 1913 until his death. He was unfit for service abroad, but was called up in June 1916 and was commissioned as a second lieutenant in an anti-aircraft battery in the Royal Garrison Artillery before transferring to the Intelligence

Department of the War Office in 1917. He died in 1932.

'The Poets are Waiting', 'Youth in Arms I', 'Youth in Arms II: Soldier', 'Youth in Arms III: Retreat' and 'Youth in Arms IV: Carrion' appeared in *Children of Love* (London: Poetry Bookshop, 1914).

Sir Henry Newbolt was born in Bilston, Staffordshire, in 1862, the son of a vicar. He was educated at Clifton College and at Corpus Christi, Oxford. He was a barrister for twelve years before dedicating himself to writing poetry and prose full-time. He was knighted in 1915, was made a Companion of Honour in 1922. He died in 1938.

'The War Films' appeared in *St. George's Day and Other Poems* (London: John Murray, 1918).

Robert Nichols was born in Shanklin on the Isle of Wight in 1893. He was educated at Winchester College and at Trinity College, Oxford, but left Oxford after a year. He was commissioned as a second lieutenant and served in the 104th Brigade of the Royal Field Artillery between October 1914 and August 1916, going to France in August 1915 but being invalided out a year later with shell shock. He subsequently worked for the ministries of Labour and Information. After the war he was Professor of English Literature at the University of Tokyo from 1921 until 1924. He died in 1944.

'Eve of Assault: Infantry Going Down to Trenches' and 'The Day's March' appeared in *Ardours and Endurances* (London: Chatto & Windus, 1917).

Wilfred Owen was born in Oswestry in 1893, the eldest son of a railway official, and was educated at the Birkenhead Institute and at Shrewsbury Technical School. In 1911 he failed the London University Matriculation Examination and became an unpaid lay assistant in an evangelical parish at Dunsden. After failing to win a scholarship to University College, Reading, he moved to France to become an English teacher. He returned to England in October 1915 and enlisted in the 28th (County of London) Battalion of the London Regiment (The Artists' Rifles), was commissioned as a second lieutenant, and was sent to join the 2nd Battalion of the Manchester Regiment in France at the end of the year. In June 1917 he was sent home on sick leave and was admitted to Craiglockhart Hospital, near Edinburgh. He was awarded the Military Cross shortly after his return to the Western Front in September 1918, and was killed on the Oise–Sambre canal on 4 November 1918.

'Anthem for Doomed Youth', 'Apologia pro Poemate Meo', 'Arms and the Boy', 'Disabled', 'Dulce et Decorum est', 'Exposure', 'Futility', 'Greater Love', 'Mental Cases', 'Smile, Smile, Smile', 'Spring Offensive', 'Strange Meeting' and 'The Send-off' appeared in *Poems by Wilfred Owen, with an Introduction by Siegfried Sassoon* (London: Chatto & Windus, 1920).

Marjorie Pickthall was born in Gunnersbury, near London, in 1883, but emigrated to Toronto in Canada in 1889. She was educated at Bishop Strachan School for Girls, and later worked in Victoria College Library at the University of Toronto. She returned to England in 1912 and lived in Bowerchalke, near Salisbury, and in London. Her wartime work included farming, training as an ambulance driver, and working in the South Kensington Meteorological Office Library. In 1920 she returned to Canada, where she died unexpectedly from an embolus in 1922. Her literary output included several hundred short stories, five novels, and several collections of poetry.

'Marching Men' appeared in *The Wood Carver's Wife and Other Poems* (Toronto: McClelland & Stewart, 1922).

Jessie Pope was born in Leicester in 1868 and was educated at Craven House, Leicester, and at North London Collegiate School. She wrote satirical fiction, verse, songs and articles for leading popular magazines and newspapers, including *Punch*, the *Daily Mail* and the *Daily Express*, and was also a writer of children's books and the first editor of Robert Tressell's socialist classic *The Ragged Trousered Philanthropists*. She lived in Fritton, Norfolk, and died in 1941.

'The Call' and 'Socks' appeared in *Jessie Pope's War Poems* (London: Grant Richards, 1915). 'The Beau Ideal' appeared in *More War Poems* (London: Grant Richards, 1915). 'War Girls' appeared in *Simple Rhymes for Stirring Times* (London: C. Arthur Pearson, 1916).

Ezra Pound was born in Idaho in 1885 and was educated at the University of Pennsylvania and at Hamilton College, New York. He came to Europe in 1908 and settled in London, becoming prominent in literary circles and founding the Imagist Movement in poetry with Richard Aldington (q.v.) and the American poet Hilda Doolittle (1886–1961). In 1920 he left England for Paris, and he subsequently settled at Rapallo, in Italy. During the Second World War he broadcast on Italian radio, and in 1945 he was charged with treason; being found unfit to plead, he was confined to a mental institution. He was released and returned to Italy in 1961. He died in 1972.

'Poem' appeared in *Umbra: The Early Poems of Ezra Pound* (London: Elkin Matthews, 1920). 'Hugh Selwyn Mauberley: V' appeared in *Hugh Selwyn Mauberley by E. P.* (London: Ovid Press, 1920).

Herbert Read was born in Kirby Moreside, Yorkshire, in 1893, the son of a brewer, and was educated at Crossley's School, Halifax, and at Leeds University. He served with the 2nd, 7th and 10th Battalions of the Yorkshire Regiment (The Green Howards) from 1915 until 1918. Initially a second lieutenant, he was made a captain in 1917 and went on to win the Military Cross and the Distinguished Service Order. Assistant keeper at the Victoria & Albert Museum between 1922 and 1931, he was also Professor of Fine Art at Edinburgh from 1931 until 1933 and editor of the *Burlington Magazine* from 1933 until 1939. He was knighted in 1953. *In Retreat* (London: L. & V. Woolf, 1925) and *Ambush* (London: Faber & Faber, 1930) are prose records of his war experiences. He died in 1968.

'My Company' appeared in *Naked Warriors* (London: Art & Letters, 1919). 'To a Conscript of 1940' appeared in *Thirty-Five Poems* (London: Faber & Faber, 1940).

[John] Edgell Rickword was born in Colchester in 1898 and joined the 28th (County of London) Battalion of the London Regiment (The Artists' Rifles) straight from school in 1916. He transferred to the 5th Battalion of the Princess Charlotte of Wales's (Royal Berkshire Regiment), was commissioned as a second lieutenant in September 1917 and was awarded the Military Cross before being invalided out of the army after losing an eye. After studying at Pembroke College, Oxford, he spent much of the 1920s as a literary critic, editing the *Calendar of Modern Letters* between 1925 and 1927, but he devoted himself to political journalism after 1930, becoming associate editor of the *Left Review* in 1934 and editor of *Our Time* from 1944 until 1947. He died in 1982.

'Moonrise over Battlefield', 'The Soldier Addresses His Body', 'Trench Poets', 'War and Peace' and 'Winter Warfare' appeared in *Behind the Eyes* (London: Sidgwick & Jackson, 1921).

Isaac Rosenberg was born in Bristol in 1890, the son of Jewish immigrants, but grew up in London. After being educated at the

353

Stepney Board School, he left at the age of fourteen to become an apprentice engraver. He attended art school in the evenings, and between 1911 and 1914 he studied at the Slade School of Art. Because of poor health, he travelled to South Africa in 1914, but returned in the following year. He originally enlisted in the 12th Battalion (Bantam) of the Suffolk Regiment (Bury St Edmunds) in October 1915, before transferring to the 12th Battalion of the South Lancashire (Prince of Wales's Volunteers) Regiment. He served on the Western Front with the 1st and 11th Battalions of the King's Own Royal Regiment (Lancaster), and was killed on 1 April 1918. His body was never recovered.

'Break of Day in the Trenches', 'Dead Man's Dump', 'Girl to Soldier on Leave', 'Louse Hunting', 'On Receiving the First News of the War', 'Returning, We Hear The Larks' and 'Soldier: Twentieth Century' appeared in *Poems by Isaac Rosenberg*, ed. Gordon Bottomley with an introductory memoir by Laurence Binyon (London: William Heinemann, 1922).

Margaret Sackville was born in 1881 at Bexhill, the daughter of the 7th Earl de la Warr, and was educated privately. A prolific poet and children's author, she joined the anti-war Union of Democratic Control in 1914 and supported it throughout the war. She lived for much of her life in Edinburgh, but died in Cheltenham in 1963.

'A Memory' appeared in *The Pageant of War* (London: Simpkin, Marshall, Hamilton, Kent & Co., 1916).

H[enry] Smalley Sarson. Nothing is known about Sarson, although when a selection of his poems was included in Galloway Kyle's *Soldier Poets: Songs of the Fighting Men* (London: Erskine Macdonald, 1916) he was described as 'Private, Canadian Contingent'.

'The Shell' appeared in *From Field and Hospital* (London: Erskine Macdonald, 1916).

Siegfried Sassoon was born at Weirleigh in Kent in 1886. He was educated at Marlborough College and at Clare College, Cambridge, but left Cambridge without a degree. He enlisted as a trooper in the Sussex Yeomanry in August 1914, and was commissioned as a second lieutenant in the 3rd Battalion of the Royal Welsh Fusiliers in May 1915. He served in France from November 1915 until August 1916, when he won the Military Cross, and again from February 1917 until April 1917, when he was invalided home with a bullet wound to his shoulder. His public protest against the continuance of the war in June led him to be sent to Craiglockhart Hospital near Edinburgh, but he returned to active service in November 1917 and served in Ireland, Palestine and France before being demobilized with the rank of captain in March 1919. He had a post-war career as a poet, novelist and memoir-writer, and wrote three semi-autobiographical works about the war: *Memoirs of a Fox-Hunting Man* (London: Faber & Gwyer, 1928), *Memoirs of an Infantry Officer* (London: Faber & Faber, 1930) and *Sherston's Progress* (London: Faber & Faber, 1936). He was awarded the CBE in 1951, and he died in 1967.

'Blighters', 'The Death-Bed', 'The Kiss', 'The Redeemer' and 'They' appeared in *The Old Huntsman and Other Poems* (London: William Heinemann, 1917). 'Banishment', 'Counter-Attack', 'In Barracks', 'Repression of War Experience' and 'Sick Leave' appeared in *Counter-Attack and Other Poems* (London: William Heinemann, 1918). 'Aftermath', 'Ancient History', 'Everyone Sang', 'Memorial Tablet' and 'Picture-Show' appeared in *Picture-Show* (New York: E. P. Dutton & Co., 1920). 'On Passing the New Menin Gate' appeared in *The Heart's Journey* (London: William Heinemann, 1928).

Alan Seeger was born in New York in 1888 and was educated at the Horace Mann School and at Harvard College. In 1912 he went to Paris to lead a bohemian life in the Latin Quarter. Three weeks after the outbreak of the war he enlisted in the French Foreign Legion, and he served on the Western Front until his death on the Somme on 4 July 1916.

'I have a rendezvous with Death' appeared in *Poems by Alan Seeger*, with an introduction by William Archer (London: Constable & Co., 1917).

Edward Shanks was born in London in 1892 and was educated at Merchant Taylors' School and at Trinity College, Cambridge. When war broke out he enlisted in the 28th (County of London) Battalion of the London Regiment (The Artists' Rifles), and in December 1914 he was commissioned as a second lieutenant in the 8th Battalion of the South Lancashire (Prince of Wales's Volunteers) Regiment. He was invalided out in April of the following year and worked for the War Office for the remainder of the war. He was the first winner of the Hawthornden Prize for imaginative writing in 1919, and was later Lecturer in Poetry at Liverpool University. He was assistant editor of the *London Mercury* from 1919 until 1922 and chief leader writer of the London *Evening Standard* between 1928 and 1935. He died in 1953.

'In Training' appeared in *Poems* (London: Sidgwick & Jackson, 1916). 'Armistice Day, 1921' appeared in *The Shadowgraph and Other Poems* (London: W. Collins Sons & Co., 1925).

Edward Shillito was born in Wakefield in 1872. Educated at Owen's College, Manchester, and at Mansfield College, Oxford, he worked as a Free Church minister in Kent, Hampshire and London. He died in 1948.

'Nameless Men' appeared in *Jesus of the Scars and Other Poems* (London: Hodder & Stoughton, 1919).

Fredegond Shove was born in Cambridge in 1889, and attended Newnham College, Cambridge, from 1910 to 1913. She died in 1949.

'The Farmer, 1917' appeared in *Dreams and Journeys* (Oxford: B. H. Blackwell, 1918).

May Sinclair was born at Rock Ferry, Cheshire, in 1863 and was educated at Cheltenham Ladies' College. A highly successful novelist and a supporter of the Women's Suffrage Movement, at the outbreak of the war she went to France, where she worked for the Motor Ambulance Unit. Sent back home after only seventeen days, she wrote an account of her experiences as *Journal of Impressions in Belgium* (London: Hutchinson & Co., 1915). After the Armistice, Sinclair became one of the leading exponents of the stream-of-consciousness novel and wrote several studies of the Brontë sisters. She died in 1946.

'Field Ambulance in Retreat' appeared in *King Albert's Book: A Tribute to the Belgian King and People from Representative Men and Women Throughout the World* (London: The Daily Telegraph in conjunction with the Daily Sketch, the Glasgow Herald and Hodder & Stoughton, 1914).

Edith Sitwell was born in Scarborough in 1887. She was the daughter of Sir George and Lady Ida Sitwell, and spent her childhood at the family seat at Renishaw Hall, Derbyshire. From 1916 until 1921 she edited *Wheels*, an annual anthology of modern poetry. She was made a Dame of the British Empire in 1954, and died ten years later.

'The Dancers' appeared in *Clown's Houses* (Oxford: B. H. Blackwell, 1918).

Osbert Sitwell was born in London in 1892, and was the brother of Edith Sitwell (q.v.). He was educated at Eton, and enlisted in the Reserve Battalion of the Grenadier Guards in 1912. In December 1914 he was transferred to the 1st Battalion, later seeing active service with the 2nd Battalion, but blood poisoning in the spring of 1916 kept him out of further action for the rest of the war. He helped his sister edit *Wheels*, and was an extremely prolific writer, publishing short stories, poems and novels throughout his life. He died in 1969.

'The Next War', 'Peace Celebrations', 'Ragtime' and 'Therefore is the name of it called Babel' appeared in *Argonaut and Juggernaut* (London: Chatto & Windus, 1919).

Soldiers' songs. Because these songs were orally transmitted, it is impossible to arrive at any definitive text. Two collections of soldiers' songs which proved useful in the preparation of these versions are John Brophy and Eric Partridge's *The Long Trail: What the British Soldier Sang and Said in the Great War of 1914–18* (London: André Deutsch, 1965) and Max Arthur's *When This Bloody War is Over: Soldiers' Songs of the First World War* (London: Piatkus, 2001).

Charles Hamilton Sorley was born in 1895 in Aberdeen and was educated at Marlborough College. He spent six months in Germany before the outbreak of war, and won a scholarship to University College, Oxford, but the declaration of hostilities saw him taking up a commission as a second lieutenant in the 7th Battalion of the Suffolk Regiment instead. He went to France in May 1915, and by August he held the rank of captain. He was killed in action at Loos on 13 October 1915.

'All the hills and vales along', 'To Germany', 'Two Sonnets' and 'When you see millions of the mouthless dead' appeared in *Marlborough and Other Poems* (Cambridge: Cambridge University Press, 1916).

J[ohn] C[ollings] Squire was born in Plymouth in 1884 and was educated at Blundell's School and at St John's College, Cambridge. He was literary editor then acting editor of the *New Statesman* between 1913 and 1918, and stood as a Labour candidate for Cambridge University in 1918, where he lost his deposit. He founded the *London Mercury* in 1919 and edited it until 1934, combining his duties with a successful career as a poet, parodist, essayist and anthologist. He was knighted in 1933, and he died in 1958.

'The Dilemma' appeared in *The Survival of the Fittest and Other Poems* (London: George Allen & Unwin, 1916). 'A Generation (1917)' appeared in *Poems: First Series* (London: Hodder & Stoughton, 1918).

Edward Thomas was born in London in 1878 and was educated at St Paul's School and at Lincoln College, Oxford. He worked as an essayist and reviewer, and under the influence of his friend Robert Frost (q.v.) he began to write poetry soon after the outbreak of the war. In July 1915 he enlisted as a private in the 28th (County of London) Battalion of the London Regiment (The Artists' Rifles), and he was commissioned as a second lieutenant in the 244th Siege Battery of the Royal Garrison Artillery a year later. He had been in France for only three months when he was killed in action at Arras on 9 April 1917.

'A Private' appeared under the pseudonym Edward Eastaway in *An Annual of New Poetry 1917* (London: Constable & Co., 1917). 'As the Team's Head-Brass', 'Lights Out' and 'The Trumpet' appeared in *Poems by Edward Thomas ('Edward*

Eastaway') (London: Selwyn & Blount, 1917). 'This is no case of petty Right or Wrong' appeared in *Last Poems* (London: Selwyn & Blount, 1918).

W[alter] J[ames] Turner was born in Melbourne, Australia, in 1889 and was educated at Scotch College, Adelaide. He came to London in 1906, and served in the Royal Garrison Artillery between 1916 and 1918. He was music critic of the *New Statesman* from 1916 until 1940 and the drama critic of the *London Mercury* between 1919 and 1923. He succeeded Siegfried Sassoon (q.v.) as literary editor of the *Daily Herald* in 1920, and from 1942 he was the literary editor of *The Spectator*. He died in 1946.

'Men Fade Like Rocks' and 'The Navigators' appeared in *In Time Like Glass* (London: Sidgwick & Jackson, 1921).

Francis Brett Young was born in Halesowen, Worcestershire, in 1884 and was educated at Epsom College and at Birmingham University. A doctor by profession, he served with the Royal Army Medical Corps in East Africa, with the rank of major, but was eventually invalided home with fever and exhaustion; *Marching on Tanga* (London: W. Collins Sons & Co., 1917) is an account of his wartime experiences. After the war, he had a successful career as a novelist, dramatist and author of travel books, dying in 1954.

'Song of the Dark Ages' and 'The Pavement' appeared in *Poems 1916–1918* (London: W. Collins Sons & Co., 1919).

Further Reading

ANTHOLOGIES OF
FIRST WORLD WAR POETRY

Wartime Anthologies

Andrews, Lieutenant C. E., ed., *From the Front: Trench Poetry* (New York: D. Appleton & Co., 1918)

Clark, G. H., ed., *A Treasury of War Poetry* (London and New York: Houghton, Mifflin, 1917)

Collins, V. H., ed., *Poems of War and Battle* (Oxford: Clarendon Press, 1914)

A Crown of Amaranth: Being a Collection of Poems to the Memory of the Brave and Gallant Gentlemen Who Gave Their Lives for Great and Greater Britain (London: Erskine Macdonald, 1915)

Elliott, H. B., ed., *Lest We Forget: A War Anthology* (London: Jarrolds, 1915)

Halliday, W. J., ed., *Pro Patria: A Book of Patriotic Verse* (London: J. M. Dent & Sons, 1915)

Kyle, Galloway, ed., *Soldier Poets: Songs of the Fighting Men* (London: Erskine Macdonald, 1916)

——, ed., *Soldier Poets: More Songs by the Fighting Men* (London: Erskine Macdonald, 1917)

Leonard, R. M., ed., *Patriotic Poems* (Oxford: Oxford University Press, 1914)

Lloyd, Bertram, ed., *Poems Written during the Great War 1914–1918: An Anthology* (London: George Allen & Unwin, 1918)

Macklin, Alys Eyne, ed., *The Lyceum Book of War Verse* (London: Erskine Macdonald, 1918)

Manning-Foster, A. E., ed., *Lord God of Battles: A War Anthology* (London: Cope & Fenwick, 1914)

Osborn, E. B., ed., *The Muse in Arms: A Collection of War Poems, for the Most Part Written in the Field of Action, by Seamen, Soldiers and Flying Men Who Are Serving, or Have Served in the Great War* (London: John Murray, 1917)

Poems of the Great War (London, Chatto & Windus, 1914)

Songs and Sonnets for England in Wartime: Being a Collection of Lyrics by Various Authors Inspired by the Great War (London: John Lane, 1914)

Tulloch, David, ed., *Songs and Poems of the Great World War* (London: Davis Press, 1915)

Later Anthologies of First World War Poetry

Black, E. L., ed., *1914–1918 in Poetry* (London: University of London Press, 1970)

Brereton, Frederick, ed., *An Anthology of War Poems* (London: Collins, 1930)

Cross, Tim, ed., *The Lost Voices of World War One* (London: Bloomsbury, 1988)

Featherstone, Simon, ed., *War Poetry: An Introductory Reader* (London: Routledge, 1995)

Gardner, Brian, ed., *Up the Line to Death: The War Poets 1914–1918* (London: Methuen, 1964)

Hibberd, Dominic, and Onions, John, eds., *Poetry of the Great War: An Anthology* (London: Macmillan, 1986)

Hussey, Maurice, ed., *Poetry of the First World War* (London: Longmans, Green & Co., 1967)

Jaquet, E. R., ed., *These Were the Men: Poems of the War, 1914–1918* (London: Marshall Bros., 1919)

Lloyd, Bertram, ed., *The Paths of Glory: A Collection of Poems Written during the War 1914–1919* (London: George Allen & Unwin, 1919)

Motion, Andrew, ed., *First World War Poems* (London: Faber & Faber, 2003)

Nichols, Robert, ed., *An Anthology of War Poetry 1914–1918* (London: Nicholson & Watson, 1943)

Parsons, I. M., ed., *Men Who March Away: Poems of The First World War* (London: Chatto & Windus, 1965)

Reilly, Catherine, ed., *Scars upon My Heart: Women's Poetry of the First World War* (London: Virago, 1981)

Roberts, David, ed., *Minds at War: Essential Poetry of the First World War in Context* (Burgess Hill: Saxon Books, 1998)

Silkin, Jon, ed., *The Penguin Book of First World War Poetry* (Harmondsworth: Allen Lane and Penguin Books, 1979)

Stephen, Martin, ed., *Never Such Innocence: A New Anthology of Great War Verse* (London: Buchan & Enright, 1988)

Taylor, Martin, ed., *Lads: Love Poetry of the Trenches* (London: Constable, 1989)

Trotter, Jacqueline, ed., *Valour and Vision* (London: Hopkinson, 1920)

CRITICAL STUDIES OF
FIRST WORLD WAR POETRY

Bergonzi, Bernard, *Heroes' Twilight: A Study of the Literature of the Great War* (Manchester: Carcanet, 1997)

Buitenhuis, Peter, *The Great War of Words: Literature as Propaganda 1914–18 and After* (London: Batsford, 1989)

Caesar, Adrian, *Taking It Like a Man: Suffering, Sexuality and the War Poets* (Manchester: Manchester University Press, 1993)

363

Graham, Desmond, *The Truth of War: Owen, Rosenberg and Blunden* (Manchester: Carcanet, 1984)

Hibberd, Dominic, ed., *Poetry of the First World War: A Casebook* (London: Macmillan, 1981)

Johnston, John H., *English Poetry of the First World War: A Study in the Evolution of Lyric and Narrative Form* (London: Oxford University Press, 1964)

Khan, Nosheen, *Women's Poetry of the First World War* (Brighton: Harvester, 1988)

Marsland, Elizabeth A., *The Nation's Cause: French, English and German Poetry of the First World War* (London: Routledge, 1991)

Parfitt, George, *English Poetry of the First World War: Contexts and Themes* (Hemel Hempstead: Harvester Wheatsheaf, 1990)

Reilly, Catherine, *English Poetry of the First World War: A Bibliography* (London: George Prior, 1978)

Roucoux, Michel, ed., *English Literature of the Great War Revisited: Proceedings of a Symposium at the University of Picardy* (Amiens: Presses de L'UER Clerc Université, 1989)

Rutherford, Andrew, *The Literature of War: Five Studies in Heroic Virtue* (London: Macmillan, 1978)

Silkin, Jon, *Out of Battle: The Poetry of the Great War* (Oxford: Oxford University Press, 1972)

Spear, Hilda D., *Remembering, We Forget: A Background Study to the Poetry of the First World War* (London: Davis-Poynter, 1979)

THE CULTURAL IMPACT OF THE FIRST WORLD WAR

Bond, Brian, *The Unquiet Western Front: Britain's Role in Literature and History* (Cambridge: Cambridge University Press, 2002)

Ecksteins, Modris, *Rites of Spring: The Great War and the Birth of the Modern Age* (London: Bantam Press, 1989)

Fussell, Paul, *The Great War and Modern Memory* (Oxford: Oxford University Press, 1975)

Hynes, Samuel, *A War Imagined: The First World War and English Culture* (London: Bodley Head, 1990)

Stephen, Martin, *The Price of Pity: Poetry, History and Myth in the Great War* (London: Leo Cooper, 1996)

Poem Acknowledgements

Richard Aldington: All poems © The Estate of Richard Aldington.

Martin Armstrong: 'Before the Battle' (1921) is reproduced from *Collected Poems* by Martin Armstrong (© Estate of Martin Armstrong 1931) by permission of PFD (www.pfd.co.uk) on behalf of the estate of Martin Armstrong.

Herbert Asquith: 'The Volunteer' included by permission of Macmillan UK.

Maurice Baring: 'August, 1918' reproduced by permission of A. P. Watt Ltd on behalf of the Trustees of the Maurice Baring Will Trust.

Laurence Binyon: Both poems appear by permission of The Society of Authors as the literary representative of the Estate of Laurence Binyon.

Edmund Blunden: 'Festubert: The Old German Line' (1916), 'The Midnight Skaters' (1925), 'At Senlis Once' (1928), 'Illusions' (1928), 'Preparations for Victory' (1928), 'Vlamertinghe: Passing the Chateau' (1928), 'Report on Experience' (1929) from *Poems of Many Years* by Edmund Blunden (© Estate of Mrs Claire Blunden 1957) and 'Ancre Sunshine' (© Estate of Mrs Claire Blunden 1968) from *Garland* magazine in July 1968 are reproduced by permission of PFD (www.pfd.co.uk) on behalf of the Estate of Mrs Claire Blunden.

Vera Brittain: 'The Superfluous Woman', 'Hospital Sanctuary' and 'The War Generation: *Ave*' by Vera Brittain from *Poems of the War and After* (1934) are included by permission of Mark Bostridge and Rebecca Williams, her literary executors.

May Wedderburn Cannan: Both poems included by kind permission of James Slater.

(www.pfd.co.uk) on behalf of the estate of Rose Macaulay
© Estate of Rose Macaulay (as printed in the original volume).

John Masefield: 'August, 1914' reprinted by permission of The
Society of Authors as the Literary Representative of the Estate
of John Masefield.

Sir Henry Newbolt: 'The War Films' appears by kind permission
of Peter Newbolt.

Robert Nichols: Both poems are included by permission of Anne
Charlton.

Jessie Pope: 'War Girls' from *Simple Rhymes for Stirring Times*
© Octopus Publishing Ltd 1916.

Edgell Rickword: All poems appear by permission of Carcanet
Press Ltd.

Siegfried Sassoon: All poems © Siegfried Sassoon by kind permis-
sion of George Sassoon.

Edward Shanks: 'Armistice Day, 1921' included by permission
of Macmillan UK.

May Sinclair: 'Field Ambulance in Retreat' is reproduced with
permission of Curtis Brown Group Ltd, London, on behalf
of the Estate of May Sinclair © May Sinclair 1914.

Edith Sitwell: 'The Dancers' is included by permission of David
Higham Associates on behalf of the author.

Osbert Sitwell: All poems appear by permission of David Higham
Associates on behalf of the author.

Francis Brett Young: Both poems are reproduced by permission
of David Higham Associates on behalf of the author.

Every effort has been made to trace copyright holders. The
publishers would be interested to hear from any copyright hold-
ers not here acknowledged.

Index of Titles and First Lines